Benedictine Book of Song II

Tobias Colgan, O.S.B.
Editor-in-Chief

Christine Manderfeld, O.S.B.
Colleen Winston, O.S.B.
Laurian Schumacher, O.S.B.
Monica Laughlin, O.S.B.
Robert Koopmann, O.S.B.
Editors

A Liturgical Press Book

THE LITURGICAL PRESS
Collegeville, Minnesota

Engraving and typography by A-R Editions, Madison, Wisconsin

Line drawings by Eric Lies, O.S.B.

Cover design by Fred Petters

Excerpts from the English translation of the *Lectionary for Mass* © 1969, 1980, 1981, International Committee on English in the Liturgy, Inc. (ICEL); the English translation of *The Roman Missal* © 1973, ICEL.

English translation of Kyrie, Gloria in Excelsis, Sanctus and Benedictus, and Agnus Dei prepared by the International Consultation on English Texts.

Selected Psalms and Scripture selections are taken from the New American Bible, copyright © 1970 by The Confraternity of Christian Doctrine, Washington, D.C.

Copyright © 1992 by The Order of St. Benedict, Inc., Collegeville, Minnesota. All rights reserved. No part of this book may be reproduced in any form or by any means, electronic or mechanical, including photocopying, recording, taping, or any retrieval system, without the written permission of The Liturgical Press, Collegeville, Minnesota 56321. Printed in the United States of America.

ISBN 0-8146-1811-1

Contents

    Contributors 7
    Introduction 9
1 Alabemos a Dios
2 All Who Seek to Know
3 Alleluia. All Peoples, Clap Your Hands
4 Almighty God, Your Word Is Cast
5 As Evening Falls
6 At This Banquet
7 Christ Is Born to Us This Day
8 Come, Gather at the Table
9 Come, Let Us to the Lord Our God
10 Come, Share This Meal and Eat
11 Cuándo, Señor, Te Llevarás Cautiva
12 Day Made Sacred
13 En la Noche las Sombras Oscuras
14 God of Mercy, God of Grace
15 God, You Call Us to This Place
16 Good and Faithful Servant
17 Great Artist of the Universe
18 Hail, Mother of Jesus
19 Hear Our Prayer, O Gentle Mother
20 Hijo del Eterno Padre
21 I Am the Vine
22 I Praise You, O God
23 I Rejoiced When I Heard Them Say
24 I Saw Water Flowing
25 I Search and Search to Find My God
26 If a Grain of Wheat Falls
27 In the Beginning God Created Heaven
28 In the Breaking of the Bread
29 Infant Wrapped in God's Own Light
30 Into the Silence of Our Hearts
31 Jesus, Come! For We Invite You
32 Let Desert Wasteland Now Rejoice
33 Let Everything Within You
34 Let the Hungry Come to Me
35 Let Us Come Before the Lord
36 Libra Mis Ojos de la Muerte
37 Lo! What a Cloud of Witnesses
38 Lord Jesus Christ, Son of David
39 Lord Jesus, As We Turn from Sin
40 Lord, It Is Good for Us to Be Here

41 Lord, You Are a Banquet
42 Merciful Redeemer, Come
43 Not in the Wind
44 Now Go, the Mass Is Ended
45 Now We Gather, Keeping Vigil
46 O Come, Bless the Lord
47 O Come, Let Us Follow
48 O Father, Lead Us Back to You
49 O Let All That Has Life
50 Oh Bondadoso Creador, Escucha
51 On Our Journey to the Kingdom
52 Out of Everlasting Stillness
53 Oye Nuestra Voz, Oh Cristo
54 Renewed in Your Great Love
55 Savior of the Nations, Come
56 Sing of Glory and His Body
57 Sing We of the Blessed Mother
58 Sing, Sing Praise to Creator God
59 Strengthened by the Body and Blood of the Lord
60 Take Courage, Have Faith
61 Teach Me the Way of Your Decrees
62 The Blazing Sun Has Run Its Course
63 The Cup of Salvation
64 The Lord Is Kind and Merciful
65 The Lord Said to My Lord
66 There Is No Greater Love
67 The Word of God
68 This Is God's Holy Temple
69 This Is the Day the Lord Has Made
70 This Is What the Lord Asks of You
71 Though the Hills Be Wrapped in Silence
72 To the Wedding Feast God Calls Us
73 Today Is Born Our Savior
74 Unto Us a Child Is Given
75 Wait When the Seed Is Planted
76 Was It Not Needful
77 We Come Before You, Lord
78 We Now Recall the Saving Death
79 We Offer Prayer in Sorrow, Lord
80 We Praise You, Lord, with Joy This Day
81 We Stand to Greet the Dawning Day
82 We Thank You, Father, Lord of All
83 What Feast of Love
84 When All the Stars of Morning Sang
85 When Evening Falls and Labors Cease

86 When from Bondage We Are Summoned
87 When Peace Like a River
88 Who Are These, Like Stars Appearing
89 You Are God, We Chant Your Praises
90 You Are the Way
91 Litany for Lent/Reconciliation
92 Litany of Mary of Nazareth
93 Litany of Saints
94 Mass in E Minor
    94a Lord, have mercy
    94b Glory to God
    94c Holy
    94d Memorial Acclamation
    94e Amen
    94f Kingdom Acclamation
    94g Lamb of God
95 Mass of Hope
    95a Lord, have mercy
    95b Glory to God
    95c Holy
    95d Memorial Acclamation
    95e Amen
    95f Lamb of God
96 Mass Ordinary XV
    96a Lord, have mercy
    96b Glory to God
    96c Holy
    96d Memorial Acclamation
    96e Amen
    96f Lamb of God
97 Mass in E
    97a Lord, have mercy
    97b Holy
    97c Memorial Acclamation
    97d Amen
    97e Lamb of God
98 Weekday Mass
    98a Gospel Acclamation (Alleluia)
    98b Gospel Acclamation (Praise—for Lent)
    98c Holy
    98d Memorial Acclamation
    98e Amen
    98g Lamb of God
99 Mass in F
    99a Holy

       99b Memorial Acclamation
       99c Amen
       99d Lamb of God
100 Missa Simplex
       100a Holy
       100b Memorial Acclamation
       100c Amen
       100d Lamb of God
101 Mass of St. Benedict
       101a Holy
       101b Memorial Acclamation
       101c Amen
       101d Lamb of God
102 Eucharistic Acclamations
       102a Holy
       102b Memorial Acclamation
       102c Amen
103 Glory to God
104 Glory Be to God on High
105 a Alleluia
     b Alleluia
     c Alleluia
106 Alleluia. Hail, O Highly Favored One
107 Alleluia. I Call You My Friends
108 Alleluia. Your Words, O Lord
109 Holy (Felicitas)
110 a Memorial Acclamation C
     b Memorial Acclamation D
111 Lamb of God
112 Lamb of God
       Liturgical Index
       Topical Index

Contributors

Abadía Benedictina de San José, Güigüe, Venezuela
 Jesus-Maria Sasía, O.S.B.; S. Axpe, O.S.B.; S. Azkue, O.S.B.

Assumption Abbey, Richardton, N.D.
 Aaron Jensen, O.S.B.

Conception Abbey, Conception, Mo.
 Gary Poole and Aelred Rosser, O.S.B.; Kilian Sullivan, O.S.B.;
 Timothy Schoen, O.S.B.

Monasterio Benedictino de las Condes, Santiago, Chile
 León Tolosa, O.S.B.

Mount St. Mary's Abbey, Wrentham, Mass.
 Edith Scholl, O.C.S.O.; Miriam Pollard, O.C.S.O.

Sacred Heart Monastery, Yankton, S.D.
 Jane Klimisch, O.S.B.

St. Anselm Abbey, Manchester, N.H.
 Matthew Leavy, O.S.B.

St. Anselm Abbey, Washington, D.C.
 Isaac Borocz, O.S.B.

St. Bede Abbey, Peru, Ill.
 Mark Strassburger, O.S.B.

St. Benedict's Convent, St. Joseph, Minn.
 Cecile Gertken, O.S.B.; Christine Manderfeld, O.S.B.; Delores Dufner, O.S.B.;
 Ellen Cotone, O.S.B.; Terri Nehl, O.S.B.

St. Gregory Abbey, Shawnee, Okla.
 Damian Whalen, O.S.B.

St. John's Abbey, Collegeville, Minn.
 Henry Bryan Hays, O.S.B.; Robert Koopmann, O.S.B.

St. Joseph Abbey, St. Benedict, La.
 Aelred Kavanagh, O.S.B.; Dominic Braud, O.S.B.; Sean Duggan, O.S.B.

St. Louis Abbey, St. Louis, Mo.
 Ralph Wright, O.S.B.

St. Mary's Abbey, Morristown, N.J.
 Francis Muench, O.S.B.

St. Meinrad Archabbey, St. Meinrad, Ind.
 Aurelius Boberek, O.S.B.; Harry Hagan, O.S.B.; Tobias Colgan, O.S.B.

St. Placid Priory, Lacey, Wash.
 Monika Ellis, O.S.B.

St. Scholastica Priory, Duluth, Minn.
  Monica Laughlin, O.S.B.; Timothy Kirby, O.S.B.

St. Vincent Archabbey, Latrobe, Penn.
  Becket Gerald Senchur, O.S.B.

Westminster Abbey, Mission, British Columbia, Canada
  Basil Foote, O.S.B.

Jay Hunstiger, Medina, Minn.

Robert LeBlanc, Madison, Wis.

Introduction

1966 was a significant year for American Benedictine musicians. The Second Vatican Council had ended, and liturgical reforms were taking root and beginning to flower. Like others facing the exhilarating challenge of this transition, Benedictines quickly realized the need for creating liturgical compositions that resonated with the changing times.

Against this background was founded the group that has come to be known as the Benedictine Musicians of the Americas. Since 1966, American Benedictine men and women have freely shared their musical compositions and liturgical texts with each other. These works, like earthenware pottery, are formed from the clay of monastic spirituality and fired in the kiln of daily liturgical prayer.

Early on it became apparent that many of the compositions were of such quality that they needed to be shared with others. With that goal in mind, the first *Benedictine Book of Song* was published in 1980 on the occasion of the 1500th anniversary of the birth of SS. Benedict and Scholastica. It was a collection of hymns, service music, and responsorial psalms composed by Benedictines from throughout the United States. This present volume, which marks the twenty-fifth anniversary of the establishment of the Benedictine Musicians of the Americas, follows closely in the footsteps of its predecessor.

The introduction to the first volume notes that "although this is music composed by monks and sisters, the selections are written for everyone." In choosing materials for *Benedictine Book of Song II*, the editorial team has kept this principle firmly in mind. "Written for everyone" does not necessarily mean "easy," of course. Some of the melodies may take more practice than others, but we think it will be practice time well spent.

Like its predecessor, *Benedictine Book of Song II* contains hymns for seasons, feasts, and rites of the Church, many being suitable for use at the Liturgy of the Hours as well as at celebrations of the Eucharist. Seven of the hymns are in Spanish, for which non-metric translations are provided. There are also a number of Mass settings, several responsorial psalms, and three litanies.

Unlike its predecessor, *Benedictine Book of Song II* posed more of a challenge in regard to language issues. The past eleven years have seen a heightened awareness not only of horizontal (people) language, but also of vertical (God) language. Concerning the former, the editorial team has tenaciously held to the principles of inclusive language. Regarding God language, the team requested that contributors submit texts portraying God in terms that are not exclusively masculine. To some degree this has been achieved.

The editorial team was overwhelmed by the response to our request for compositions. Over 550 pieces were submitted! We are grateful to all who sent us their work and are especially pleased that this book represents the work of thirty-one contributors from the United States, Canada, and Venezuela.

The team is likewise grateful to Jim Zychowicz and Janet Huenink at A-R Editions for their courteous attention throughout the music engraving process. We also wish to thank Fr. Michael Naughton, director of The Liturgical Press, and the staff of the Press for its encouragement and support.

Finally, I would like to pay tribute to the other members of the editorial team. It has been one of the finest collaborative experiences of my life: professional, thorough, and very rewarding. I'm sure the others will join me in singling out Sr. Laurian Schumacher, O.S.B., for a solo bow. Her secretarial skills and proofreading ability, along with her great tenacity, have gone a long way toward making this book what it is.

And now the book is in your hands. May it be for you an instrument of joyful praise for many years to come.

> Tobias Colgan, O.S.B.
> Editor-in-Chief
>
> First Sunday of Advent, 1991

Alabemos a Dios 1

1. A - la - be - mos a Dios que en su Pa - la - bra
2. No ce - rre - mos el al - ma a su lla - ma - da
3. Ca - mi - ne - mos los dí - as de es - ta vi - da
4. Je - sús Tú nos di - jis - te e - ras ca - mi - no

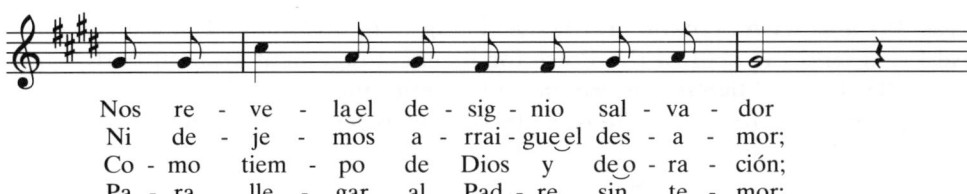

Nos re - ve - la el de - sig - nio sal - va - dor
Ni de - je - mos a - rrai - gue el des - a - mor;
Co - mo tiem - po de Dios y de o - ra - ción;
Pa - ra lle - gar al Pad - re sin te - mor;

Y di - ga - mos en sú - pli - ca con - fia - da
Aun - que du - ra es la lu - cha, su pa - la - bra
El es fiel a la a - lian - za pro - me - ti - da:
Con - cé - de - nos la gra - cia de tu Es - pí - ri - tu

Re - nué - va - me por den - tro mi Se - ñor.
Se - rá bál - sa - mo sua - ve en el do - lor.
"Si e - res mi pueb - lo, Yo se - ré tu Dios".
Que nos lle - ve al en - cuen - tro del Se - ñor. A - men.

1. Let us praise God who in his Word
   reveals to us his saving plan
   and let us confidently request:
   "Renew me interiorly, my Lord."

2. Let us not close our soul to his call
   nor let indifference take root:
   Although the battle is hard, his word
   will be soothing balm in pain.

3. Let us walk the days of this life
   as a time of God and of prayer;
   He is faithful to the promised covenant:
   "If you are my people, I will be your God."

4. Jesus, you told us that you were the way
   to come to the Father without fear;
   Grant us the grace of your Spirit
   that it may bring us to meet the Lord.

Text: © Conferencia Episcopal de Colombia, Secretariado de Liturgia; Non-metrical tr. Tobias Colgan, O.S.B. © 1989 St. Meinrad Archabbey, St. Meinrad, IN 47577
Music: S. Azkue, O.S.B. © 1987 Abadía Benedictina de San José, Güigüe, Venezuela; acc. Jesús M. Sasía, O.S.B. © 1989 Abadía Benedictina de San José, Güigüe, Venezuela

2 All Who Seek to Know

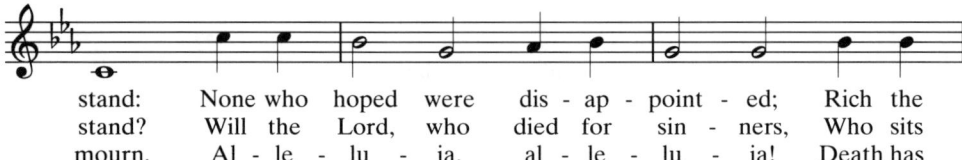

1. All who seek to know and serve God, See the past and understand: None who hoped were disappointed; Rich the blessings from God's hand! None who waited were forsaken; None who trusted were deceived. All who asked for gracious pardon, Gentle mercy have received.

2. If our God does not condemn us, Who against us then will stand? Will the Lord, who died for sinners, Who sits now at God's right hand? What could take us from Christ Jesus? Neither hunger, sword, nor pain! Neither life nor death shall part us From the Lamb for us once slain.

3. Alleluia, alleluia! Joy awaits all those who mourn. Alleluia, alleluia! Death has died and life is born. Alleluia, alleluia! Our redeemer, Jesus lives! Alleluia, alleluia! Grace and glory Jesus gives!

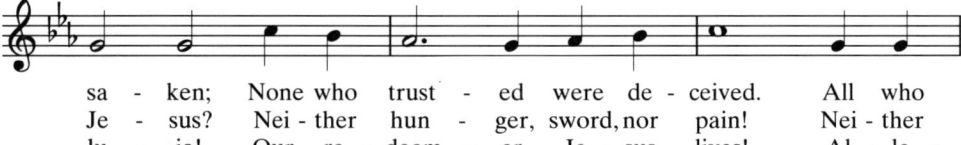

Text: Delores Dufner, O.S.B. © 1983 Sisters of St. Benedict, St. Joseph, MN 56374
Music: ©1983 Jay F. Hunstiger, 4545 Wichita Trail, Medina MN 55340

Alleluia. All Peoples, Clap Your Hands 3

REFRAIN

Al - le - lu - ia, al - le - lu - ia, al - le - lu - ia!

VERSES

1. All peo - ples, clap your hands,
2. God goes up with shouts of joy; The
3. God is king of all the earth,
4. To the Fa - ther glo - ry give,

Cry to God with shouts of joy!
Lord goes up with trum - pet blast.
Sing praise with all your skill.
And to Je - sus Christ, his Son,

For the Lord, the Most High, we must fear,
Sing praise for God, sing praise,
God is king o - ver all the na - tions;
To the Spir - it who dwells in our hearts—

Great king o - ver all the earth.
Sing praise to our king, sing praise.
God reigns on his ho - ly throne.
Both now and for - ev - er - more.

Text: Psalm 47: 2, 3, 6–9 © 1963–1986 Ladies of the Grail (England). Used by permission of GIA Publications, Inc., Chicago, IL, exclusive agent. All rights reserved.
Music: Tobias Colgan, O.S.B. © 1985 St. Meinrad Archabbey, St. Meinrad, IN 47577

4 Almighty God, Your Word Is Cast

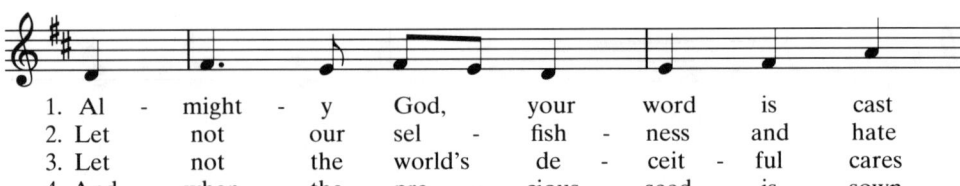

1. Al - might - y God, your word is cast
2. Let not our sel - fish - ness and hate
3. Let not the world's de - ceit - ful cares
4. And when the pre - cious seed is sown

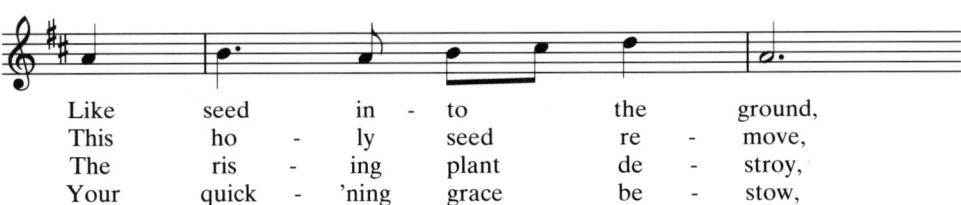

Like seed in - to the ground,
This ho - ly seed re - move,
The ris - ing plant de - stroy,
Your quick - 'ning grace be - stow,

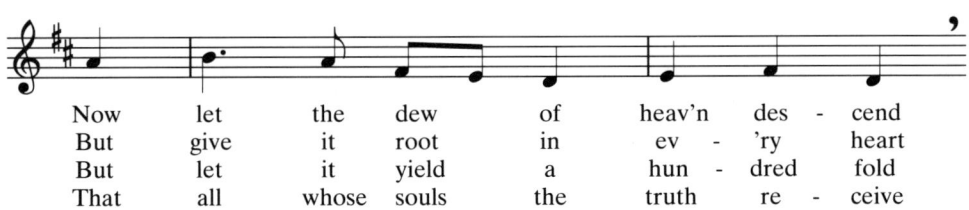

Now let the dew of heav'n des - cend
But give it root in ev - 'ry heart
But let it yield a hun - dred fold
That all whose souls the truth re - ceive

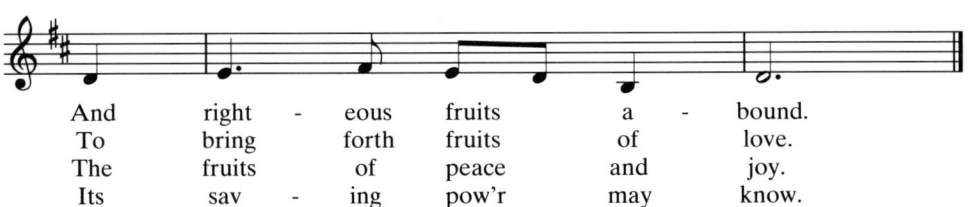

And right - eous fruits a - bound.
To bring forth fruits of love.
The fruits of peace and joy.
Its sav - ing pow'r may know.

Text: John Cawood, 1775–1852, alt.
Music: Tobias Colgan, O.S.B. © 1986 St. Meinrad Archabbey, St. Meinrad, IN 47577

As Evening Falls 5

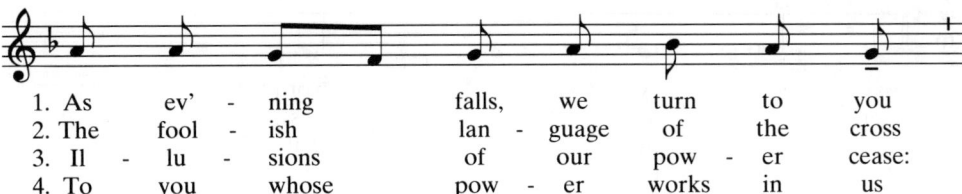

1. As ev'-ning falls, we turn to you
2. The fool-ish lan-guage of the cross
3. Il-lu-sions of our pow-er cease:
4. To you whose pow-er works in us

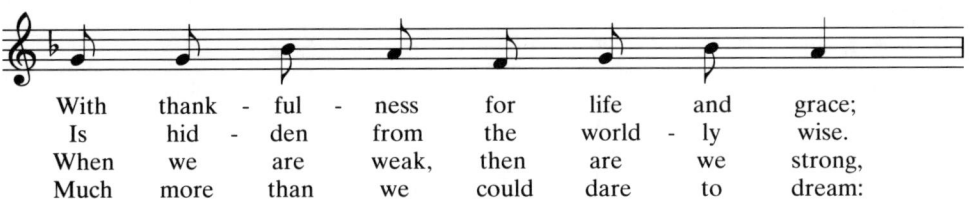

With thank-ful-ness for life and grace;
Is hid-den from the world-ly wise.
When we are weak, then are we strong,
Much more than we could dare to dream:

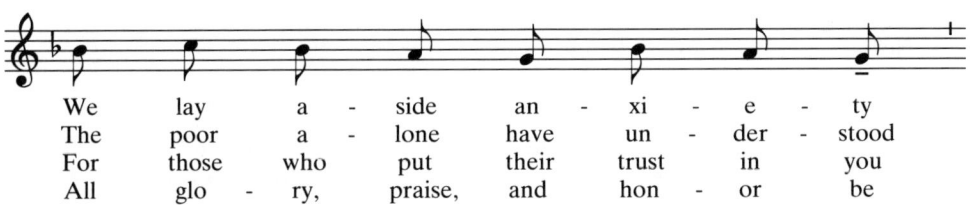

We lay a-side an-xi-e-ty
The poor a-lone have un-der-stood
For those who put their trust in you
All glo-ry, praise, and hon-or be

To rest at peace in your em-brace.
Where-in true strength and pow-er lies.
Will not for-ev-er be proved wrong.
Our song and ev-er-last-ing theme! A-men.

Text: Delores Dufner, O.S.B. © 1986 Sisters of St. Benedict, St. Joseph, MN 56374
Music: Plainchant, Mode II, LIBER HYMNARIUS; acc. Cecile Gertken, O.S.B. © 1989
Sisters of St. Benedict, St. Joseph, MN 56374

TE LUCIS ANTE TERMINUM
88 88

6 At This Banquet

REFRAIN *Confidently*

At this banquet Jesus gives us his very self. Let us draw near, though we be unworthy, To receive so great a gift.

VERSES

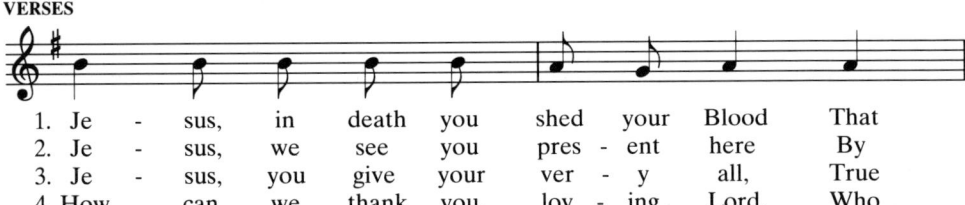

1. Jesus, in death you shed your Blood That each of us might live;
2. Jesus, we see you present here By faith and not by sight;
3. Jesus, you give your very all, True Bread from heav'n above;
4. How can we thank you, loving Lord, Who died to save mankind?

Now as our living Bread from heav'n Your loving self you give.
Love bids you welcome, living Bread, In whom is all delight.
You are the giver and the gift, The sign, the source, of love.
Take what we have, take all we are, Our heart, our strength, our mind.

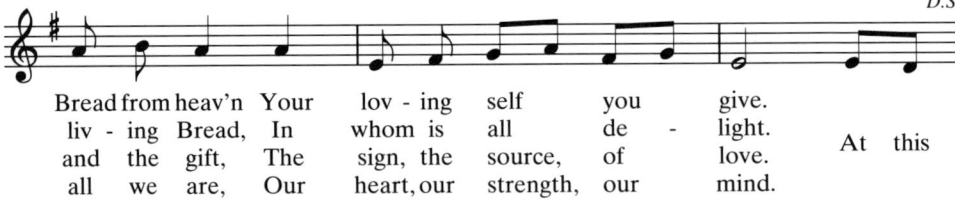

D.S.

5. These are the gifts we now restore
   To you, our Lord and King;
   Since you have shared your all with us
   To you our all we bring.

Text: Refrain: Tobias Colgan, O.S.B. © 1986 St. Meinrad Archabbey, St. Meinrad, IN 47577; vv.: © 1969 James Quinn, S.J. Reprinted by permission of Geoffrey Chapman, a division of Cassell Publishers Ltd.
Music: Tobias Colgan, O.S.B. © 1986 St. Meinrad Archabbey, St. Meinrad, IN 47577

Christ Is Born to Us This Day 7

REFRAIN *mf*
Christ is born to us this day! Re-joice!

Sing al-le-lu-ia! De-o Gra-ti-as!

VERSES

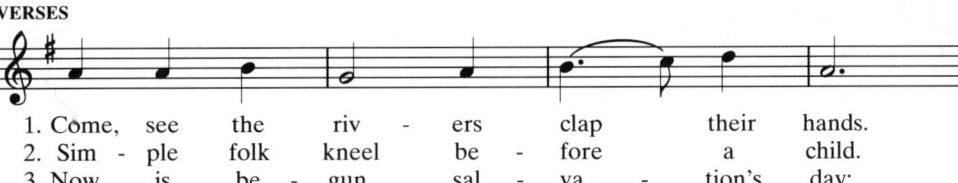

1. Come, see the riv - ers clap their hands.
2. Sim - ple folk kneel be - fore a child.
3. Now is be - gun sal - va - tion's day;

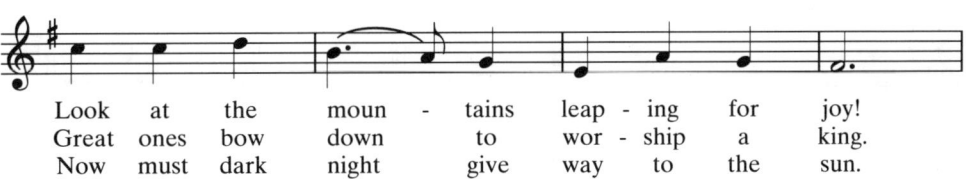

Look at the moun - tains leap - ing for joy!
Great ones bow down to wor - ship a king.
Now must dark night give way to the sun.

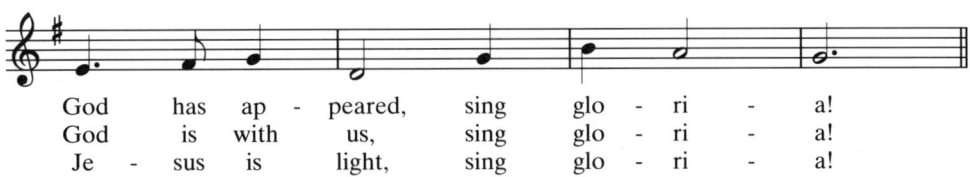

God has ap - peared, sing glo - ri - a!
God is with us, sing glo - ri - a!
Je - sus is light, sing glo - ri - a!

Text: Delores Dufner, O.S.B. © 1989 Sisters of St. Benedict, St. Joseph, MN 56374
Music: Christine Manderfeld, O.S.B. © 1989, 1991 Sisters of St. Benedict, St. Joseph, MN 56374

7a Christ Is Born to Us This Day
(Four-Part Equal Voices)

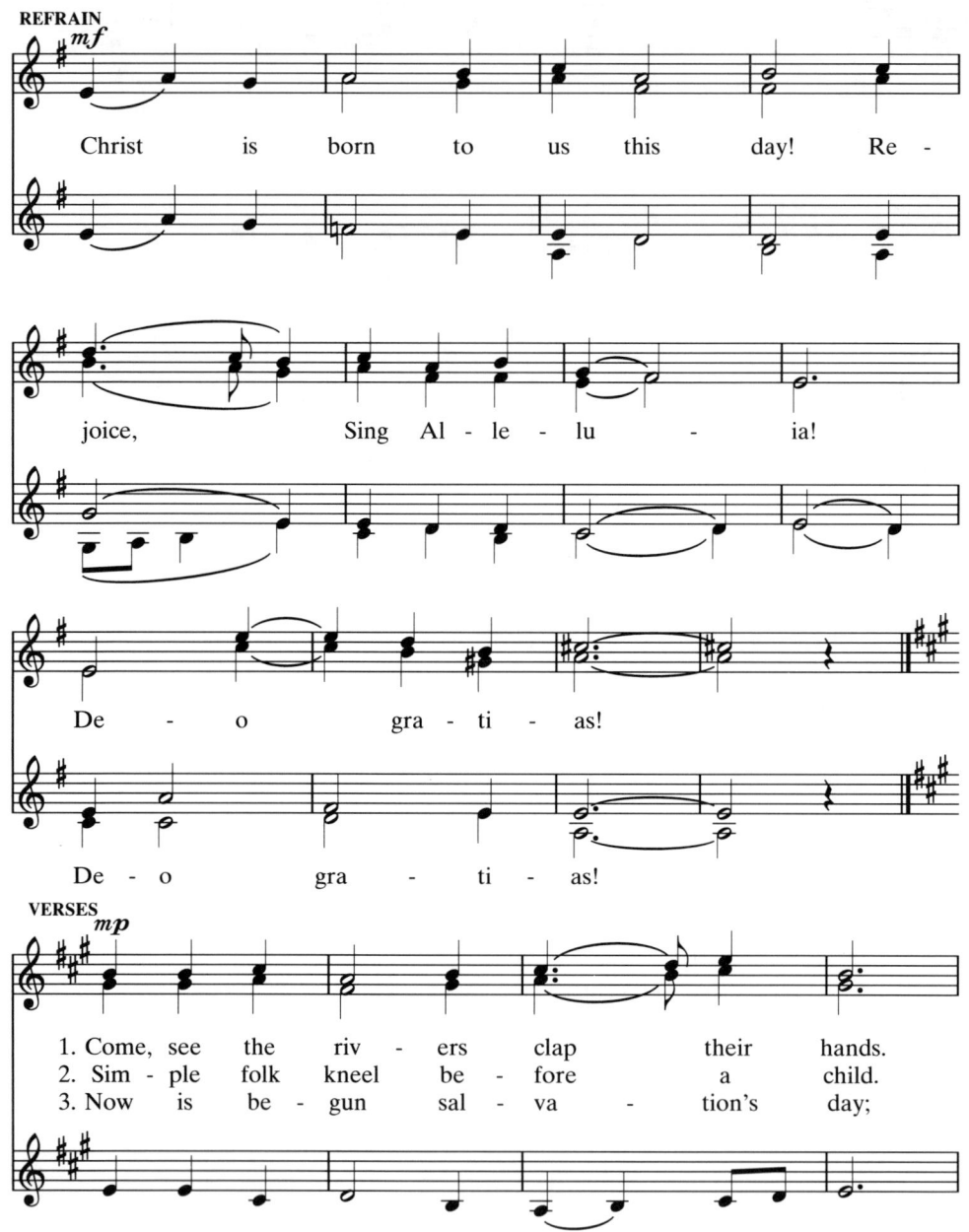

Text: Delores Dufner, O.S.B. © 1989 Sisters of St. Benedict, St. Joseph, MN 56374
Music: Christine Manderfeld, O.S.B. © 1989, 1991 Sisters of St. Benedict, St. Joseph, MN 56374

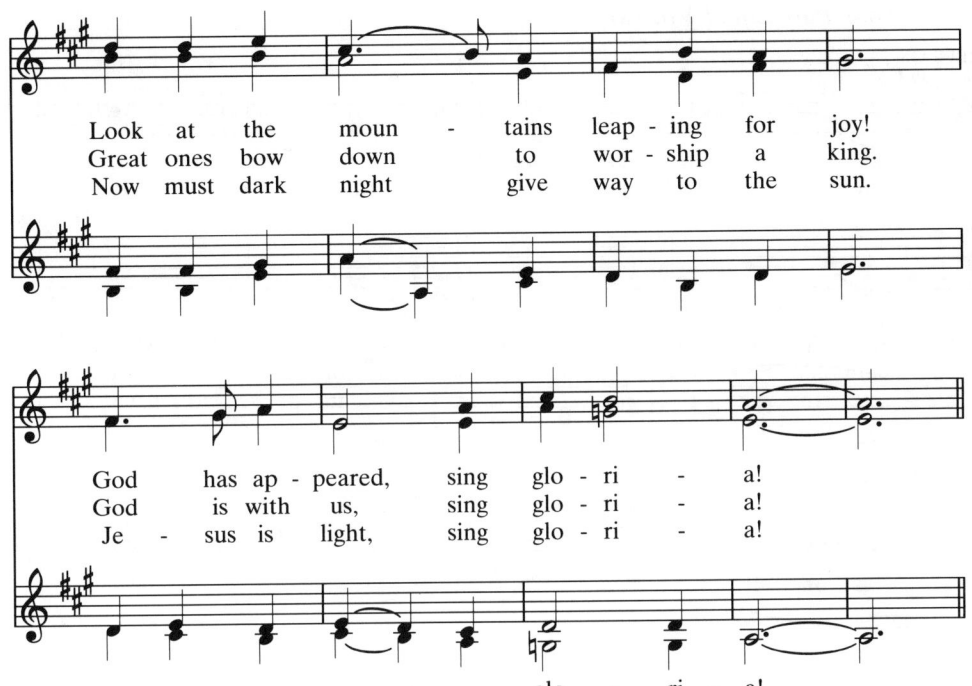

8 Come, Gather at the Table

1. Come, ga-ther at the ta-ble That Je-sus Christ has spread;
2. O come from farms and ci-ties, O come from toil and care;
3. Like flow-ers in a gar-den, We're dif-f'rent yet the same;

Come, drink the cup now of-fered, Come, eat the Ho-ly Bread.
In faith and hope now ga-ther, This feast of love to share.
We long to be u-ni-ted In love to praise God's name.

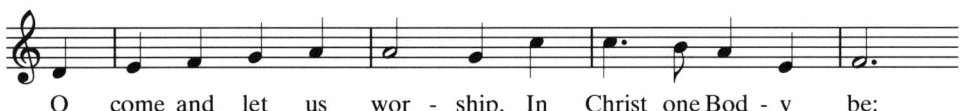

O come and let us wor-ship, In Christ one Bod-y be:

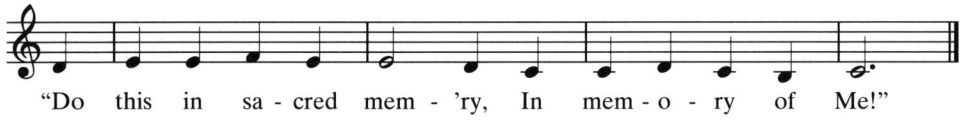

"Do this in sa-cred mem-'ry, In mem-o-ry of Me!"

Text: Jane Klimisch, O.S.B. © 1989 Sacred Heart Convent, Yankton, SD 57078
Music: Samuel S. Wesley, 1810–1876; alt. acc. Jane Klimisch, O.S.B. © 1989 Sacred Heart Convent, Yankton, SD 57078

AURELIA
76 76 D

Come, Let Us to the Lord Our God 9

1. Come, let us to the Lord our God   With con-trite hearts re-turn,
2. Long has the night of sor-row reigned,   The dawn shall bring us light;
3. As dew up-on the ten-der herb,   Dif-fus-ing fra-grance round;

Our God is gra-cious, nor will leave   The des-o-late to mourn.
God shall ap-pear, and we shall rise   With glad-ness in his sight.
As show'rs that ush-er in the spring,   And cheer the thirst-y ground:

God's voice com-mands the tem-pest forth,   And stills the storm-y wave;
Our hearts, if God we seek to know,   Shall know and then re-joice;
So shall his pres-ence bless our souls,   And shed a joy-ful light;

And though his arm be strong to smite,   'Tis al-so strong to save.
This com-ing like the morn shall be,   Like morn-ing songs God's voice.
That hal-lowed morn shall chase a-way   The sor-rows of the night.

Text: Isaac Watts, 1674–1748, alt.
Music: Robert LeBlanc © 1982 St. Joseph Abbey, St. Benedict, LA 70457

HOSEA
86 86 D

9a Come, Let Us to the Lord Our God

(Two-Part Equal Voices, unaccompanied)

1. Come, let us to the Lord our God With con-trite hearts re-turn,
2. Long has the night of sor-row reigned, The dawn shall bring us light;
3. As dew up-on the ten-der herb, Dif-fus-ing fra-grance round;

Our God is gra-cious, nor will leave The des-o-late to mourn.
God shall ap-pear, and we shall rise With glad-ness in his sight.
As show'rs that ush-er in the spring, And cheer the thirst-y ground:

God's voice com-mands the tem-pest forth, And stills the storm-y wave;
Our hearts, if God we seek to know, Shall know and then re-joice;
So shall his pres-ence bless our souls, And shed a joy-ful light;

And though his arm be strong to smite, 'Tis al-so strong to save.
This com-ing like the morn shall be, Like morn-ing songs God's voice.
That hal-lowed morn shall chase a-way The sor-rows of the night.

Text: Isaac Watts, 1674–1748, alt.
Music: Robert LeBlanc © 1982 St. Joseph Abbey, St. Benedict, LA 70457

HOSEA
86 86 D

Come, Share This Meal and Eat 10

REFRAIN

Come, share this meal and eat, for my flesh is real food, my

blood is real drink. Come, and I will give you life.

VERSE 1

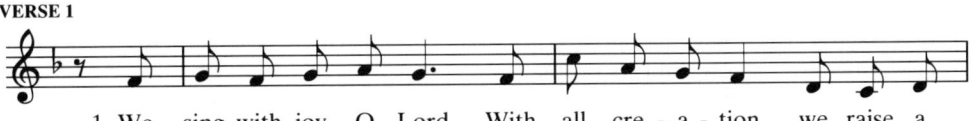
1. We sing with joy O Lord. With all cre-a-tion we raise a

song of praise to your ho-ly name.

VERSES 2–4

2. We tell your won-ders, Lord. With all your ho-ly peo-ple,
3. We eat your bod-y, Lord. With all the church we join in
4. Grant us your peace, O Lord. With faith re-newed and lives made

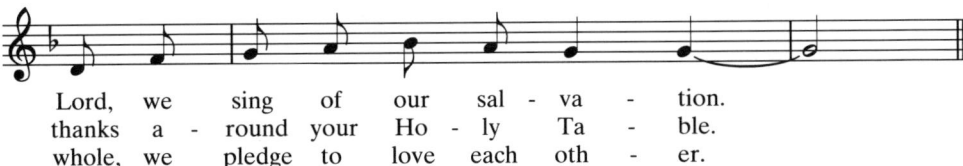
Lord, we sing of our sal-va-tion.
thanks a-round your Ho-ly Ta-ble.
whole, we pledge to love each oth-er.

Text: Damian S. Whalen, O.S.B. © 1985 St. Gregory Abbey, Shawnee, OK 74801
Music: Damian S. Whalen, O.S.B. © 1985 St. Gregory Abbey, Shawnee, OK 74801

11 Cuándo, Señor, Te Llevarás Cautiva

1. ¿Cuándo, Señor, te llevarás cautiva
2. ¿Cuándo, también, emprenderá su vuelo,
3. ¿Cuándo, Señor, los gritos de los hombres
4. Y ¿Cuándo, finalmente, Padre amado,

la historia de pecado que el mundo concibió?;
la débil esperanza de nuestro corazón?;
serán clamor eterno de júbilo y de paz?;
seremos en el Hijo tus hijos de adopción?;

¿Cuándo, Señor, serán cielos y tierra
¿Cuándo, Señor, florecerán en el barro
¿Cuándo, Señor, las penas y tristezas
¿Cuándo, Señor, será ya todo en todos

el cielo de tu amor?
tu sangre y tu pasión?
tu gloria alumbrarán?
tu Espíritu de amor? A - mén.

1. When, Lord, will you take captive
the history of sin the world conceived?
When, Lord, will the heavens and earth
be the heaven of your love?

2. When also will embark on its flight
the feeble hope of our heart?
When, Lord, will flower in the clay
your blood and your passion?

3. When, Lord, will people's cries
be the eternal cry of joy and peace?
When, Lord, will your glory
enlighten pain and sadness?

4. And when, finally, beloved Father,
will we be adopted children in the Son?
When, Lord, will your Spirit of love
be all in all?

Text: © Conferencia Episcopal de Colombia, Secretariado de Liturgia; Non-metrical tr. Tobias Colgan, O.S.B. © 1989 St. Meinrad Archabbey, St. Meinrad, IN 47577
Music: S. Axpe, O.S.B. © 1987 Abadía Benedictina de San José, Güigüe, Venezuela; acc. Jesús M. Sasía, O.S.B. © 1989 Abadía Benedictina de San José, Güigüe, Venezuela

Day Made Sacred   12

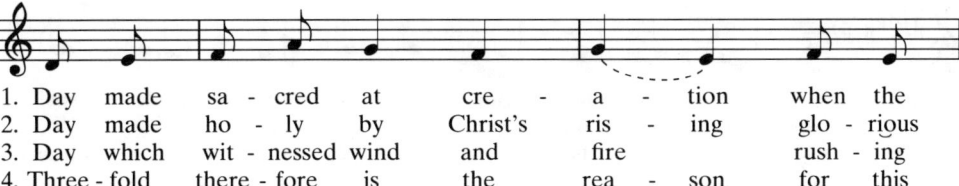

1. Day made sa - cred at cre - a - tion when the
2. Day made ho - ly by Christ's ris - ing glo - rious
3. Day which wit - nessed wind and fire rush - ing
4. Three - fold there - fore is the rea - son for this

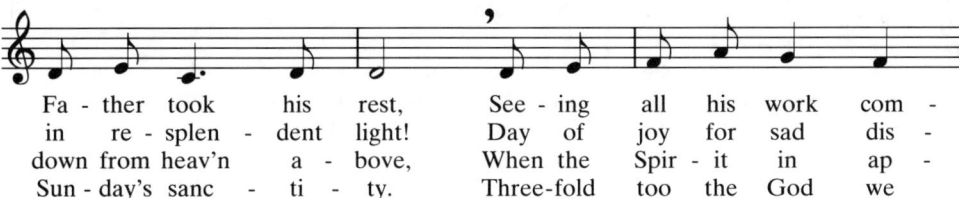

Fa - ther took his rest, See - ing all his work com -
in re - splen - dent light! Day of joy for sad dis -
down from heav'n a - bove, When the Spir - it in ap -
Sun - day's sanc - ti - ty. Three-fold too the God we

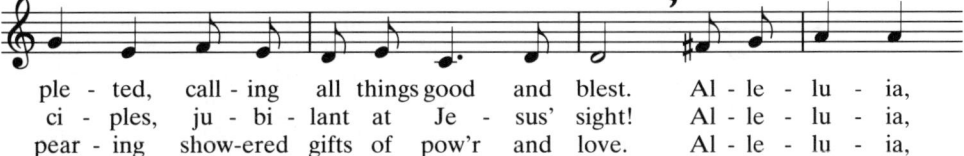

ple - ted, call - ing all things good and blest. Al - le - lu - ia,
ci - ples, ju - bi - lant at Je - sus' sight! Al - le - lu - ia,
pear - ing show-ered gifts of pow'r and love. Al - le - lu - ia,
wor - ship, now and for e - ter - ni - ty. Al - le - lu - ia,

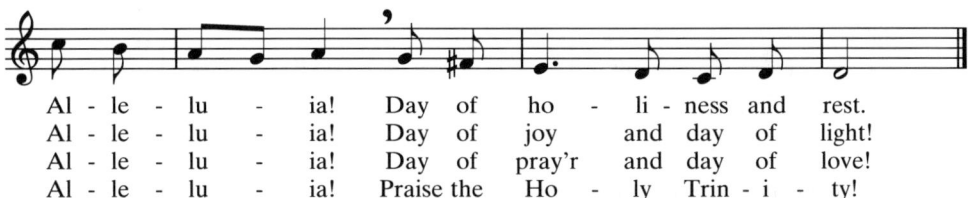

Al - le - lu - ia! Day of ho - li - ness and rest.
Al - le - lu - ia! Day of joy and day of light!
Al - le - lu - ia! Day of pray'r and day of love!
Al - le - lu - ia! Praise the Ho - ly Trin - i - ty!

Text: Matthew Leavy, O.S.B. © 1986 St. Anselm Abbey, Manchester, NH 03102
Music: Robert LeBlanc © 1983 St. Joseph Abbey, St. Benedict, LA 70457

COVENANT
87 87 87

13 En la Noche las Sombras Oscuras

1. During the night the dark shadows
   bring us fears and doubts,
   when the sun with its light awakes us
   none remain.

2. At the cradle of the day which is being born
   the loving night cried like a mother
   and in the weeping of frost and dew
   left its message.

3. You Lord of night and day,
   of stars and suns, the sun of life,
   enlighten the path of the one
   on pilgrimage to you.

4. In the night and in the soul's doubting
   you will be bright morning star,
   midday filled with blues *(literally the color)*
   and sun of hope.

5. Let us humbly adore the Father
   and let the soul sing
   to the Son and Spirit
   with never-ending hymns
   of rejoicing.

Text: © Conferencia Episcopal de Colombia, Secretariado de Liturgia; Non-metrical tr. Tobias Colgan, O.S.B. © 1989 St. Meinrad Archabbey, St. Meinrad, IN 47577
Music: S. Azkue, O.S.B. © 1987 Abadía Benedictina de San José, Güigüe, Venezuela; acc. Jesús M. Sasía, O.S.B. © 1989 Abadía Benedictina de San José, Güigüe, Venezuela

God of Mercy, God of Grace 14

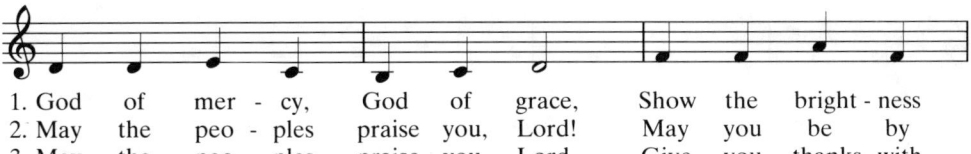

1. God of mer - cy, God of grace, Show the bright - ness
2. May the peo - ples praise you, Lord! May you be by
3. May the peo - ples praise you, Lord, Give you thanks with

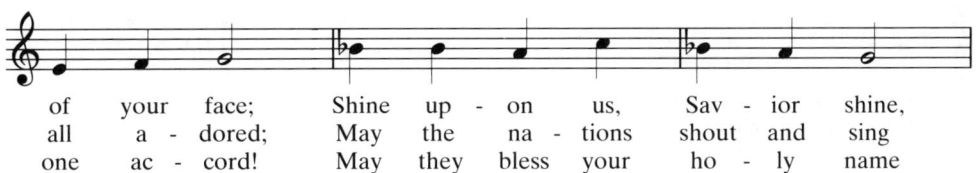

of your face; Shine up - on us, Sav - ior shine,
all a - dored; May the na - tions shout and sing
one ac - cord! May they bless your ho - ly name

Fill your Church with light div - ine, And your sav - ing
Glo - ry to their Sav - ior King, At your feet their
And your good - ness e'er pro - claim, All be - low and

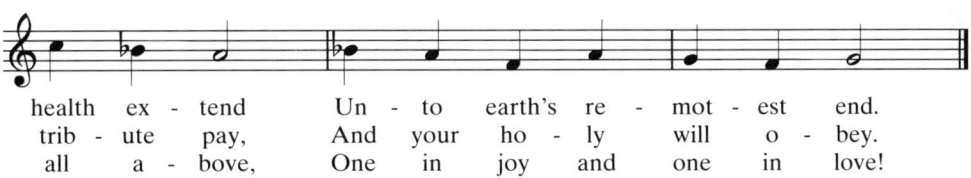

health ex - tend Un - to earth's re - mot - est end.
trib - ute pay, And your ho - ly will o - bey.
all a - bove, One in joy and one in love!

Text: Henry F. Lyte, 1793–1847, alt.
Music: Becket Gerald Senchur, O.S.B. © 1979 St. Vincent Archabbey, Latrobe, PA 15650

15 God, You Call Us to This Place

1. God, you call us to this place, So to share your love and grace.
2. Now as-sem-bled in Christ's name All your mer-cies to pro-claim,
3. In the wa-ter we were born Of the Spir-it in the Son.

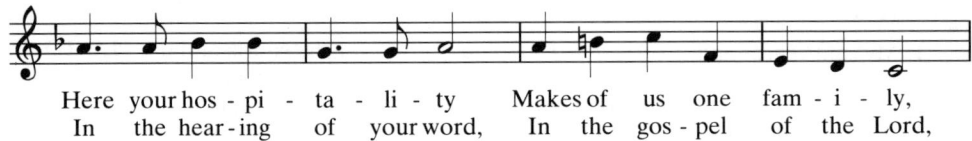

Here your hos-pi-ta-li-ty Makes of us one fam-i-ly,
In the hear-ing of your word, In the gos-pel of the Lord,
Now a priest-ly, roy-al race, Rich in ev-'ry gift of grace,

Makes our rich di-ver-si-ty Rich-er still in u-ni-ty,
In the break-ing of the bread, In the meal where we are fed,
Called, for-giv-en, loved, and freed, For the world we in-ter-cede:

Makes our ma-ny voic-es one, Joined in praise with Christ your Son.
In the Spir-it let us be One in faith and u-ni-ty.
Gath-er in-to u-ni-ty All the hu-man fam-i-ly.

Text: Delores Dufner, O.S.B. © 1987 Sisters of St. Benedict, St. Joseph, MN 56374
Music: George Job Elvey, 1816–1893.

ST. GEORGE'S WINDSOR
77 77 D

Good and Faithful Servant 16

ANTIPHON

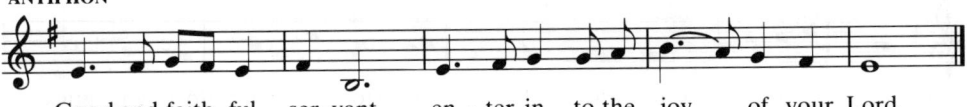

Good and faith-ful ser-vant, en - ter in to the joy of your Lord.

VERSES

1. My soul yearns and   pines   for the courts of the   LORD.
2. Happy they who dwell in your   house!   continually they   praise you.
3. I had rather one day in your   courts   than a thousand   elsewhere;
4. For a sun and a shield is the LORD God;   grace and glory he be - stows;

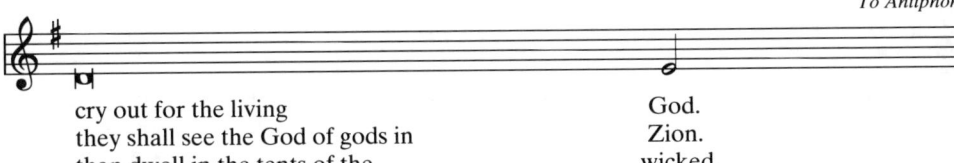

My heart and my   flesh
They go from strength to   strength;
I had rather lie at the threshold of the house of my   God
The LORD withholds no   good thing

To Antiphon

cry out for the living   God.
they shall see the God of gods in   Zion.
than dwell in the tents of the   wicked.
from those who walk in sin -   cerity.

Text: Refrain: Isaac Borocz, O.S.B. © 1982 St. Anselm's Abbey, Washington, DC 20017. Translation of psalm from the New American Bible, copyright © 1970 by the Confraternity of Christian Doctrine, Washington, DC 20017
Music: Isaac Borocz, O.S.B. © 1982 St. Anselm's Abbey, Washington, DC 20017

17 Great Artist of the Universe

1. Great artist of the universe, Of land and sea and
2. O gracious giver of all good, Of warmth and food and
3. Consoling presence in our pain And shelt'ring dusk of

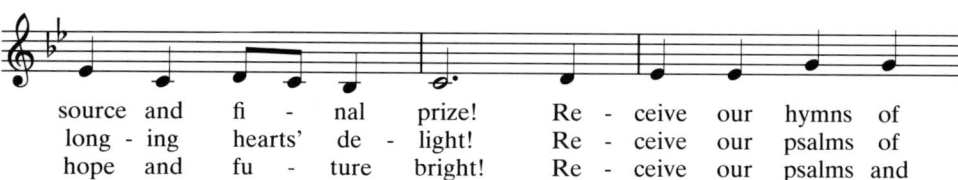

skies, Creator God of all that is, Our
light, O ever-flowing stream of love, Our
night, Transforming radiance of the dawn, Our

source and final prize! Receive our hymns of
longing hearts' delight! Receive our psalms of
hope and future bright! Receive our psalms and

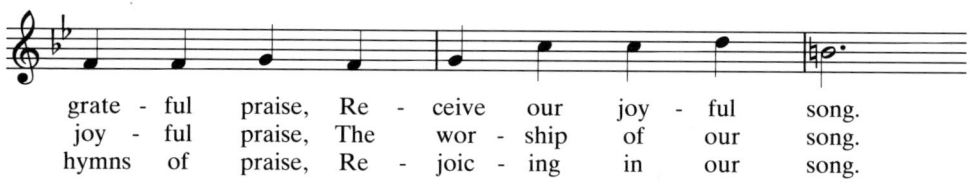

grateful praise, Receive our joyful song.
joyful praise, The worship of our song.
hymns of praise, Rejoicing in our song.

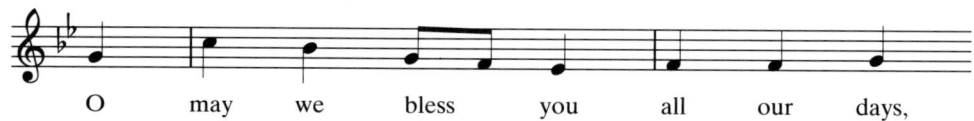

O may we bless you all our days,

Give thanks our whole life long!

Text: Delores Dufner, O.S.B. © 1987 Sisters of St. Benedict, St. Joseph, MN 56374
Music: Terri Nehl, O.S.B. © 1987 Sisters of St. Benedict, St. Joseph, MN 56374;
acc. Ellen Cotone, O.S.B. © 1987 Sisters of St. Benedict, St. Joseph, MN 56374

86 86 D

Hail, Mother of Jesus 18

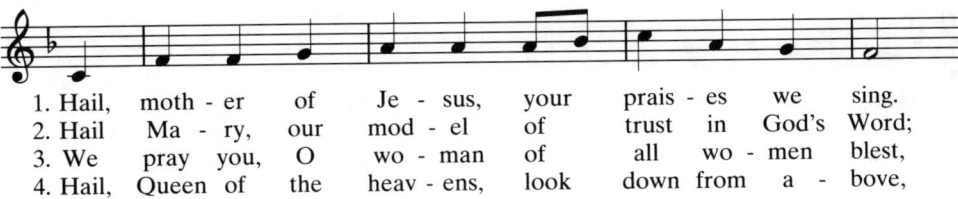

1. Hail, moth-er of Je-sus, your prais-es we sing.
2. Hail Ma-ry, our mod-el of trust in God's Word;
3. We pray you, O wo-man of all wo-men blest,
4. Hail, Queen of the heav-ens, look down from a-bove,

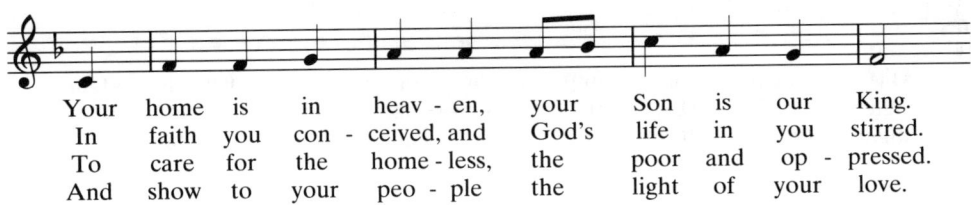

Your home is in heav-en, your Son is our King.
In faith you con-ceived, and God's life in you stirred.
To care for the home-less, the poor and op-pressed.
And show to your peo-ple the light of your love.

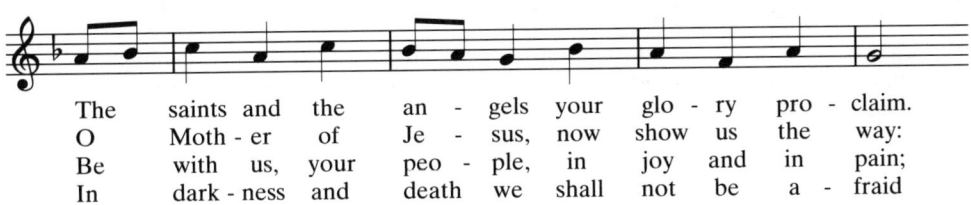

The saints and the an-gels your glo-ry pro-claim.
O Moth-er of Je-sus, now show us the way:
Be with us, your peo-ple, in joy and in pain;
In dark-ness and death we shall not be a-fraid

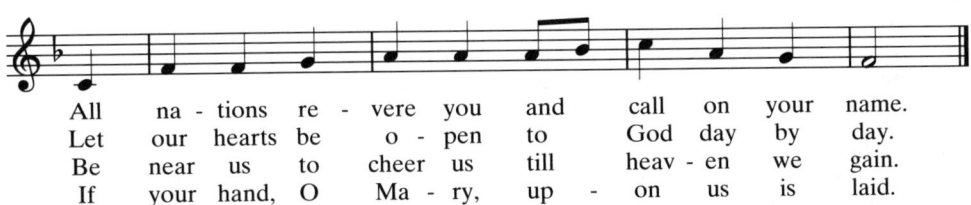

All na-tions re-vere you and call on your name.
Let our hearts be o-pen to God day by day.
Be near us to cheer us till heav-en we gain.
If your hand, O Ma-ry, up-on us is laid.

5. Hail, Virgin and Mother of all mothers blest,
To you our glad praises and pray'rs are addressed.
God's holy creation now clothed with the sun,
O pray for the churches, that all may be one!

6. To Father eternal, our anthems we raise.
To Son and to Spirit, re-echo the praise.
So gracious forever, our God three-in-One,
By all of creation, all honor be done!

Text: Adapt. Delores Dufner, O.S.B. © 1987 Sisters of St. Benedict, St. Joseph, MN 56374

MARIA ZU LIEBEN
11 11 D

19 Hear Our Prayer, O Gentle Mother

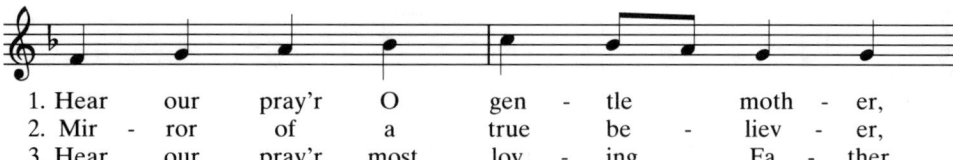

1. Hear our pray'r O gentle mother,
2. Mirror of a true believer,
3. Hear our pray'r, most loving Father,

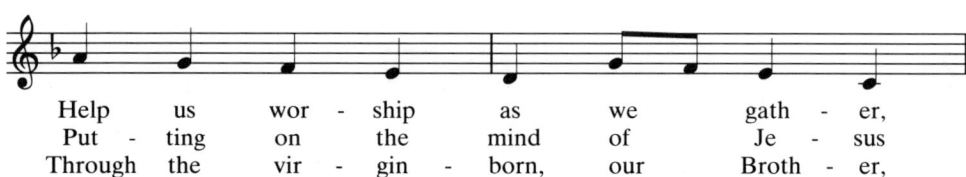

Help us worship as we gather,
Putting on the mind of Jesus
Through the virgin-born, our Brother,

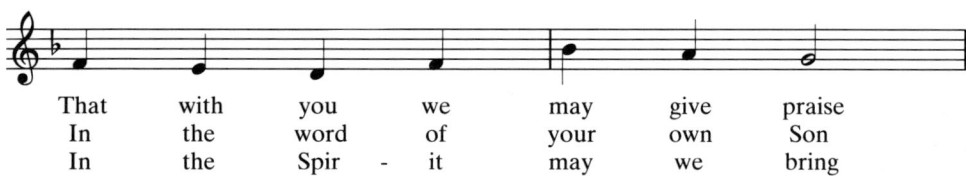

That with you we may give praise
In the word of your own Son
In the Spirit may we bring

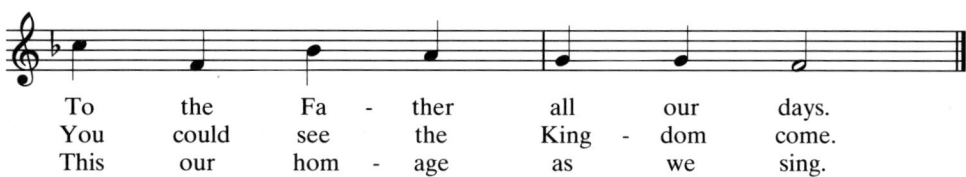

To the Father all our days.
You could see the Kingdom come.
This our homage as we sing.

(January 1)
4. Woman, raised above all nations,
   Chosen out of all creation,
   Mary, you have brought to birth
   Jesus, Lord of all the earth.

(May 31)
6. As your cousin comes to greet you
   'Blest of women,' so she greets you.
   John, who leaps within her womb,
   Knows the Bridegroom will come soon.

(September 15)
8. Mary, standing still and grieving
   As your Son in pain hung bleeding,
   You have known within your heart
   All the torment of the dark.

(March 25)
5. Humbly you received the greeting
   Brought by Gabriel to your dwelling.
   Though in darkness you believed,
   Through the Spirit you conceived.

(August 15)
7. Sinless Mary, you were taken
   By your Son from earth to heaven.
   Raised beyond our death you plead
   For your children in their need.

(December 8)
9. Mary, virgin, sinless mother,
   Humble, pow'rful, full of wonder,
   Help us have the calm to see
   What your Son calls us to be.

Text: Ralph Wright, O.S.B. vv. 1–6, 8, 9 © 1989 GIA Publications, Inc. Chicago, IL 60638; v. 7 © St. Louis Abbey, St. Louis, MO 63141
Music: G. Ch. Störl, fl. 1710

SOLLT ES GLEICH BISWEILEN SCHEINEN
88 77

Hijo del Eterno Padre 20

1. Son of the eternal Father,
   Glorious King and Redeemer,
   You transfigure humanity
   according to your image, Lord.

2. You took human form
   from the virgin Mother,
   in order to repair the damage
   of the infernal enemy.

3. For our sake you offered
   the pains of the cross
   and poured out your blood,
   the price of our salvation.

4. Now raised up you receive
   glory and honor from the Father:
   from you we await safely
   glorious resurrection.

5. Lord, be our living
   and eternal paschal joy,
   and the children of your grace
   take with you in your triumphant ascent.

6. May glory be rendered to you
   who have triumphed over death;
   to the Spirit and the Father
   may adoration be paid.

Text: © Conferencia Episcopal de Colombia, Secretariado de Liturgia; Non-metrical tr. Tobias Colgan, O.S.B. © 1989 St. Meinrad Archabbey, St. Meinrad, IN 47577
Music: Jesús M. Sasía, O.S.B. © 1987, 1989 Abadía Benedictina de San José, Güigüe, Venezuela.

21 I Am the Vine
Antiphon for congregation

21a I Am the Vine
Antiphon for Three-part choir and congregation
Verses for solo voice

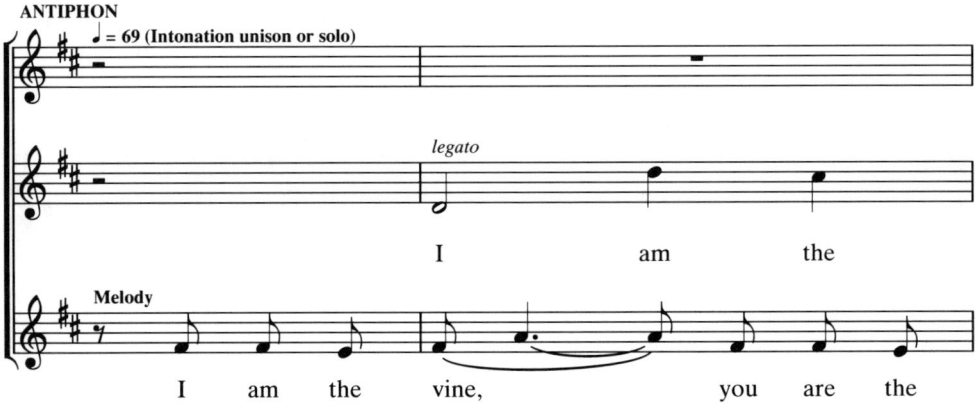

Text: Adapt. from John 15: 1-8 © 1988 Dominic Braud, O.S.B. St. Joseph Abbey, St. Benedict, LA 70457
Music: Dominic Braud, O.S.B. © 1988, St. Joseph Abbey, St. Benedict, LA 70457

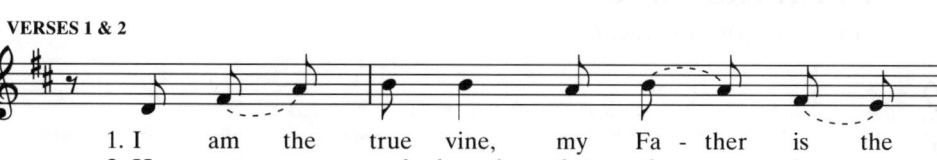

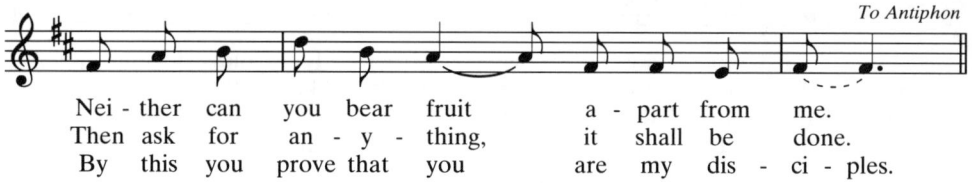

22 I Praise You, O God

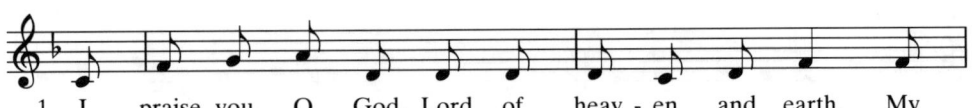

1. I praise you, O God, Lord of heav-en and earth, My
2. Mag-nif-i-cent things in my life you have done, And
3. You scat-ter the proud, but you gath-er the meek; You
4. Re-call-ing your prom-ise made a-ges a-go, You

Sav-ior, my Mak-er who called me from birth! Re-
ho-ly your name, O Com-pas-sion-ate One! From
top-ple the might-y, but strength-en the weak. The
vis-it your peo-ple, new life to be-stow. On

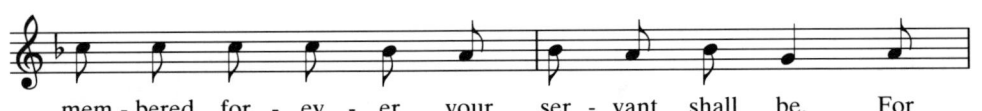

mem-bered for-ev-er your ser-vant shall be, For
past gen-er-a-tions to those yet to be, Your
rich you ig-nore, send them emp-ty a-way, But
all of your chil-dren you show-er your care, With

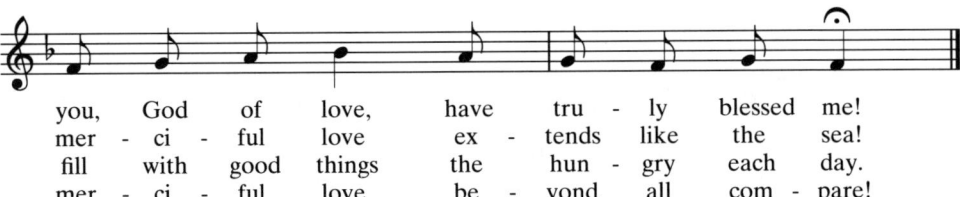

you, God of love, have tru-ly blessed me!
mer-ci-ful love ex-tends like the sea!
fill with good things the hun-gry each day.
mer-ci-ful love be-yond all com-pare!

Text: Becket Gerald Senchur, O.S.B. © 1978, 1989 St. Vincent Archabbey, Latrobe, PA 15650
Music: Becket Gerald Senchur, O.S.B. © 1978, 1989 St. Vincent Archabbey, Latrobe, PA 15650

I Rejoiced When I Heard Them Say 23

ANTIPHON

I re - joiced when I heard them say: "Let us go to the house of the

Lord." And now our feet are stand - ing with -

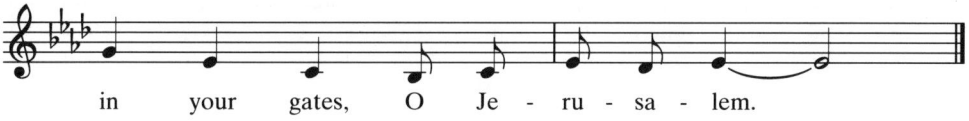

in your gates, O Je - ru - sa - lem.

VERSES

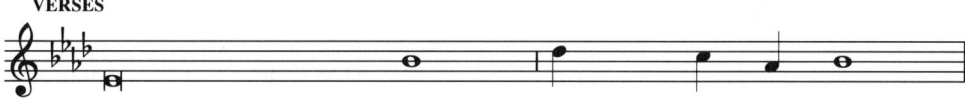

1. Jerusalem is built as a city strong - ly com - pact.
2. For Israel's law it is, there to praise the Lord's name.
3. For the peace of Jerusalem pray: "Peace be to your homes!
4. For love of my family and friends I say: "Peace up - on you!"

It is there that the tribes go up,
There were set the thrones of judgment
May peace reign in your walls,
For love of the house of the Lord

To Antiphon

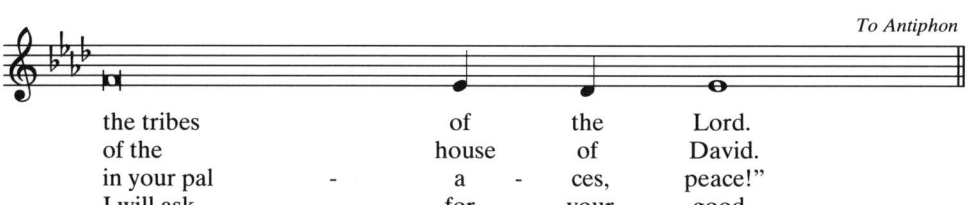

the tribes of the Lord.
of the house of David.
in your pal - a - ces, peace!"
I will ask for your good.

Text: Psalm 121 © 1963–1986, Ladies of the Grail (England). Used by permission of GIA Publications, Inc., Chicago, IL, exclusive agent. All rights reserved.
Music: Mark Strassburger, O.S.B. © 1989 St. Bede Abbey, Peru, IL 61354

24 I Saw Water Flowing

I saw water flowing from the right side of the temple, Al-le-lu-ia.

It brought God's life and salvation. And the people sang in joyful

praise, Al-le-lu-ia, Al-le-lu-ia!

Text: Based on Ezek 47:1-2, 9. From The Roman Missal, © ICEL, 1973
Music: Monica Laughlin, O.S.B. © 1986 St. Scholastica Priory, Duluth, MN 55811; acc. Robert Koopmann, O.S.B. © 1989 St. John's Abbey, Collegeville, MN 56321

I Search and Search to Find My God 25

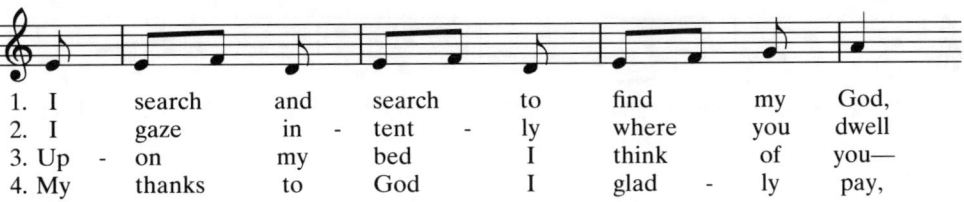

1. I search and search to find my God,
2. I gaze in-tent-ly where you dwell
3. Up-on my bed I think of you—
4. My thanks to God I glad-ly pay,

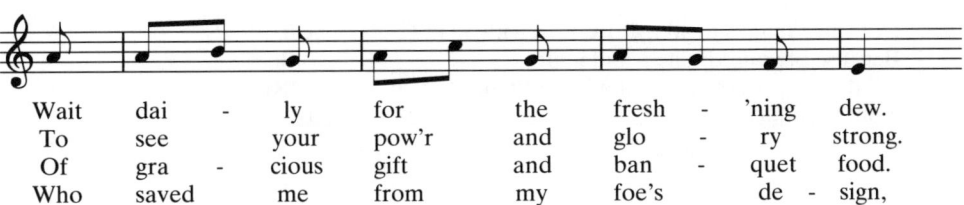

Wait dai-ly for the fresh-'ning dew.
To see your pow'r and glo-ry strong.
Of gra-cious gift and ban-quet food.
Who saved me from my foe's de-sign,

Like earth in drought, like life-less sod
I lift my hands, my lips do tell
Your shad-ow pres-ence is my help
Re-main-ing faith-ful ev-'ry day

My thirst-y soul cries out for you.
Ex-ul-tant praise of God in song.
Through mid-night watch-'s dark-ened mood.
For end-less a-ges with-out time.

Text: Monika Ellis, O.S.B. © 1983 St. Placid Priory, Lacey, WA 98506
Music: Monika Ellis, O.S.B. © 1983 St. Placid Priory, Lacey, WA 98506; acc. Tobias Colgan, O.S.B. © 1989 St. Meinrad Archabbey, St. Meinrad, IN 47577

26 If a Grain of Wheat Falls

ANTIPHON

If a grain of wheat falls to the ground and dies, it bears much fruit.

VERSES

1. I will give thanks to you, O LORD, with all my   heart,
2. Because of your kindness and your   truth,
3. All the kings of the earth shall give thanks to you, O   LORD,
4. Your right hand   saves me.

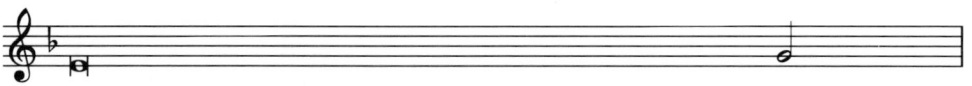

for you have heard the words of my   mouth;
for you have made great above all things your name and your   promise.
when they hear the words of your   mouth;
The LORD will complete what he has done for   me;

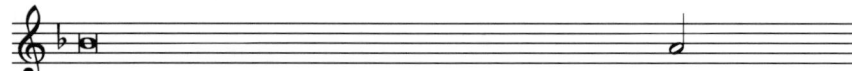

in the presence of the angels I will sing your   praise;
When I called, you answered   me;
and they shall sing of the ways of the   LORD:
your kindness, O LORD, endures for -   ever;

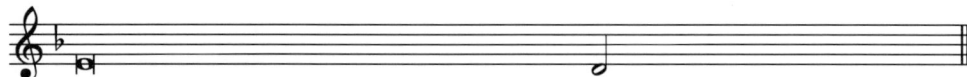

I will worship at your holy   temple.
you built up strength with -   -   in me.
"Great is the glory of the   LORD."
forsake not the work of your   hands.

Text: Refrain: Isaac Borocz, O.S.B. © 1982 St. Anselm's Abbey, Washington, DC 20017. Translation of psalm from the New American Bible, copyright © 1970 by the Confraternity of Christian Doctrine, Washington, DC 20017
Music: Isaac Borocz, O.S.B. © 1982 St. Anselm's Abbey, Washington, DC 20017

In the Beginning God Created Heaven 27

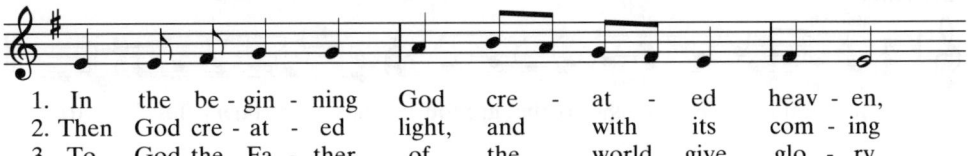

1. In the be-gin-ning God cre - at - ed heav - en,
2. Then God cre-at-ed light, and with its com - ing
3. To God the Fa - ther of the world give glo - ry,

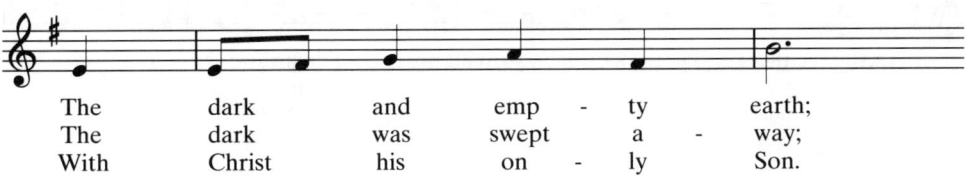

The dark and emp - ty earth;
The dark was swept a - way;
With Christ his on - ly Son.

The Spir - it moved a - cross the som - ber wa - ters
The morn - ing came, and then the qui - et ev' - ning:
Who with the Spir - it gov - ern all cre - a - tion:

And sum - moned life to birth.
The end of God's first day.
Blest Trin - i - ty in One.

Text: © 1974 Stanbrook Abbey, Worcester, England, adapt.
Music: Aaron Jensen, O.S.B. © 1980 Assumption Abbey, Richardton, ND 58652

28 In the Breaking of the Bread

ANTIPHON (Cantor/All)

In the break-ing of the bread, we have come to know the Lord,

And in drink-ing from the cup, we have shared the life of God.

VERSES:

1. As we gath-er in the Lord, As we hear the sto-ries told,
2. As we share the ho-ly meal And re-mem-ber Christ the Lord,
3. With the rich-es of this feast Hun-gry hearts are sat-is-fied,
4. Man-y grains be-come one loaf; Man-y grapes be-come the wine.
5. At this ban-quet of the Lord We re-mem-ber and give praise

To Antiphon

In the sto-ry of the cross Our life's mean-ing will un-fold.
As we eat and drink in faith, Bonds of love will be re-stored.
As with joy-ful lips we sing Praise for Je-sus glo-ri-fied.
Let us, then, one bod-y be, Who at this one ta-ble dine.
For the gra-cious love of God, Ov-er-flow-ing all our days.

Text: Delores Dufner, O.S.B. © 1988, 1989 Sisters of St. Benedict, St. Joseph, MN 56374
Music: Christine Manderfeld, O.S.B. © 1988, Sisters of St. Benedict, St. Joseph, MN 56374

Alternate verses to Hymn no. 28
(Text for Easter Season)

In the Breaking of the Bread 28a

1. As we walk the dusty road,
   Sharing all our doubts and fears,
   Someone joins us on the way,
   Gives us hope in place of tears.

2. As we gather in the Lord,
   As we hear the stories told,
   In the story of the cross
   Our life's meaning will unfold.

3. As we travel on life's way,
   All our faith in Christ restored,
   In the joy of Easter light
   We shall meet the Risen Lord.

4. At this table of the Lord
   We remember and give praise
   For the gracious love of God
   Overflowing all our days.

5. Let us, as we walk the road,
   Meet the stranger as a friend;
   Let us, with the Risen Lord,
   Travel till our journey's end.

29 Infant Wrapped in God's Own Light

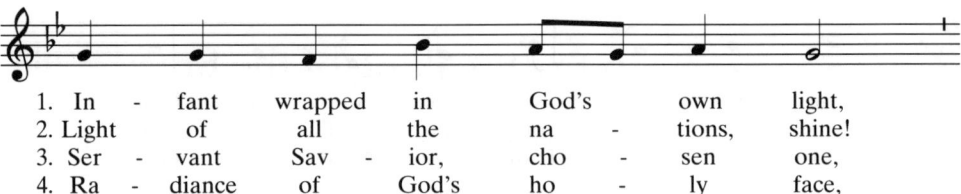

1. In-fant wrapped in God's own light,
2. Light of all the na-tions, shine!
3. Ser-vant Sav-ior, cho-sen one,
4. Ra-diance of God's ho-ly face,

Sav-ior sent to con-quer night,
Show to us who wait a sign.
You are God's be-lov-ed Son.
Shine your love in ev-'ry place.

King be-fore whom kings bowed low,
God on earth, our host and guest,
Let your Spir-it on us rest;
Splen-dor of God's glo-ry bright,

Let a star be-fore us go!
Be in flesh made man-i-fest.
Be in us made man-i-fest.
Lead us to e-ter-nal light!

Text: Delores Dufner, O.S.B. © 1984 Sisters of St. Benedict, St. Joseph, MN 56374
Music: J. Walther, Geistliche Gesangbüchlein, Wittenberg, 1524; acc. © 1984
Jay F. Hunstiger, 4545 Wichita Trail, Medina, MN 55340

NUN KOMM DER HEIDEN HEILAND
77 77

Into the Silence of Our Hearts 30

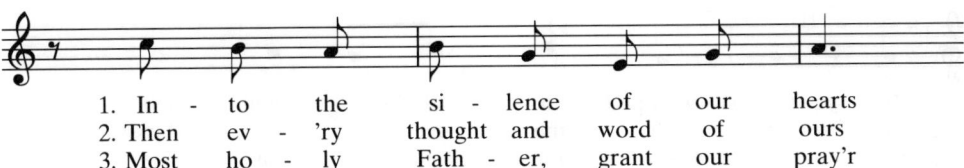

1. In - to the si - lence of our hearts
2. Then ev - 'ry thought and word of ours
3. Most ho - ly Fath - er, grant our pray'r

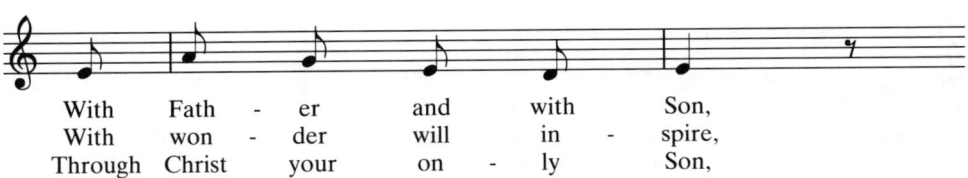

With Fath - er and with Son,
With won - der will in - spire,
Through Christ your on - ly Son,

In an - swer to our con - stant pray'r,
And all will find in us that love
That in your Spir - it we may live

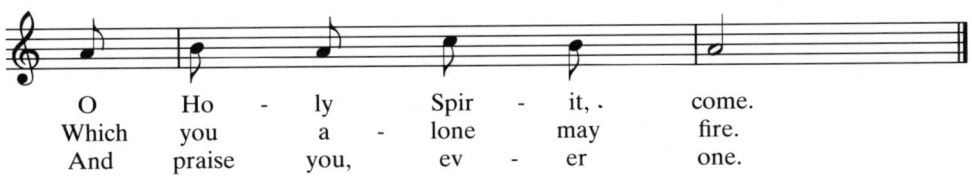

O Ho - ly Spir - it, come.
Which you a - lone may fire.
And praise you, ev - er one.

Text: Nunc Sancte nobis Spiritus; asc. to St. Ambrose, 340-397; tr. Ralph Wright, O.S.B. © 1989 GIA Publications, Inc. Chicago, IL.
All rights reserved.
Music: Tobias Colgan, O.S.B. © 1989 St. Meinrad Archabbey, St. Meinrad, IN 47577

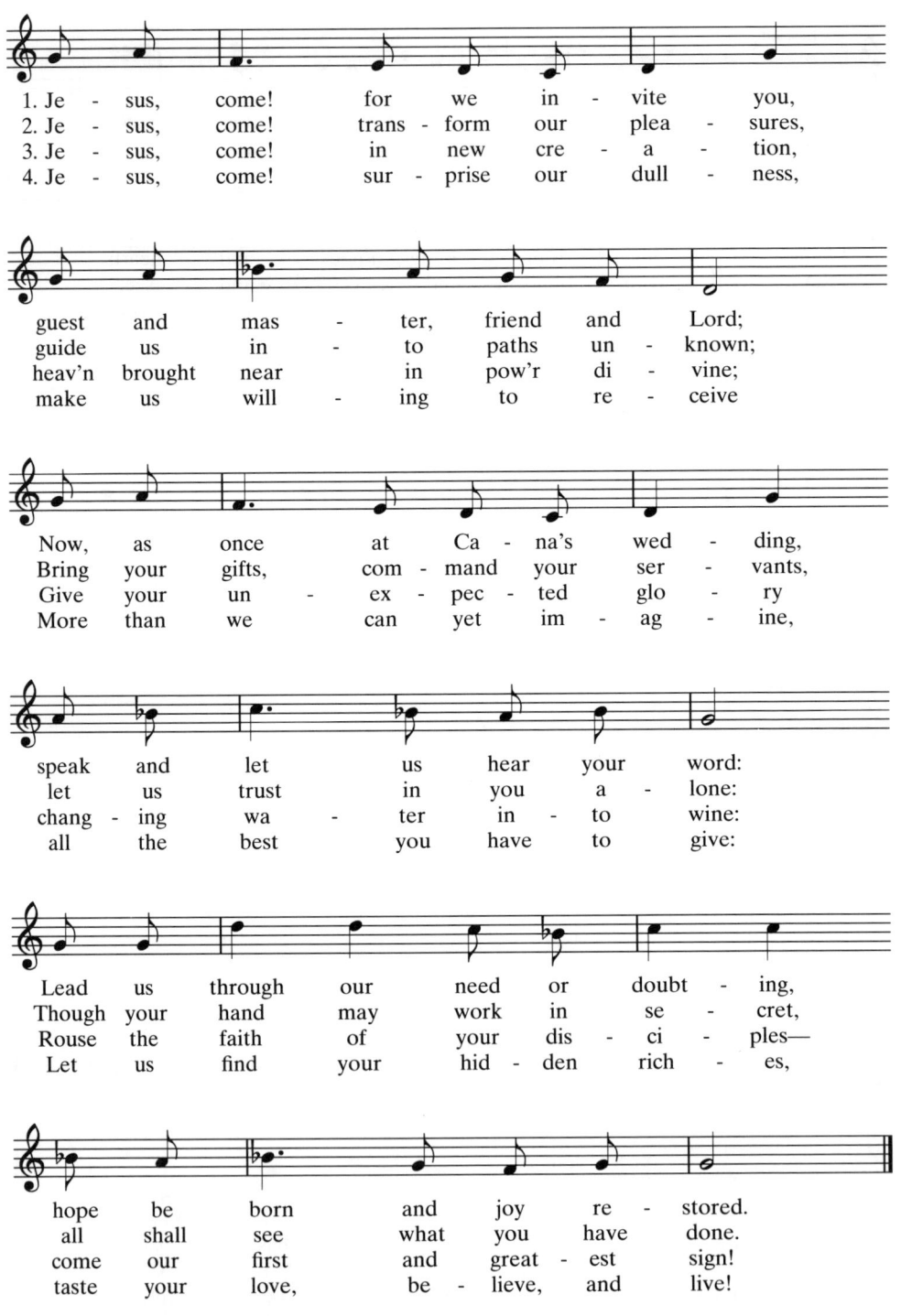

33 Let Everything Within You

ANTIPHON

Let ev-'ry-thing with-in you keep watch and wait,

for the Lord our God draws near.

VERSES

1. To you, O Lord, I lift up my   soul.
2. Lord, make me know your   ways.
3. In you I hope all day   long
4. The Lord is good and   upright.

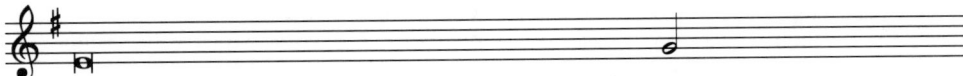

I trust you, let me not be disap - pointed.
Lord, teach me your   paths.
because of your goodness, O   Lord.
The Lord shows the path to those who   stray,

Those who hope in you shall not be disap - pointed,
Make me walk in your truth, and   teach me;
Remember your mercy,   Lord,
May innocence and uprightness pro - tect me:

but only those who wantonly break   faith.
for you are God my   Savior.
and the love you have shown from of   old.
for my hope is in you, O   Lord.

Text: Antiphon: Isaac Borocz, O.S.B. © 1982 St. Anselm's Abbey, Washington, DC 20017; vv.: Psalm 24: 1, 2a, 3; 4, 5; 5b, 6; 8,21 alt. © 1963–1986, Ladies of the Grail (England). Used by permission of GIA Publications, Inc., Chicago, IL, exclusive agent. All rights reserved.
Music: Isaac Borocz, O.S.B. © 1982 St. Anselm's Abbey, Washington, DC 20017

Let the Hungry Come to Me 34

1. Let the hun-gry come to me, Let the poor be fed.
2. I my-self am liv-ing bread; Feed on me and live.
3. Here a-mong you shall I dwell, Mak-ing all things new.
4. Nour-ished by the Word of God, Now we eat the Bread.

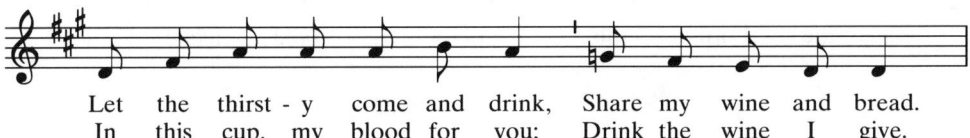

Let the thirst-y come and drink, Share my wine and bread.
In this cup, my blood for you; Drink the wine I give.
You shall be my ve-ry own, I, your God-with-you.
With the gift of God's own life Hun-gry hearts are fed.

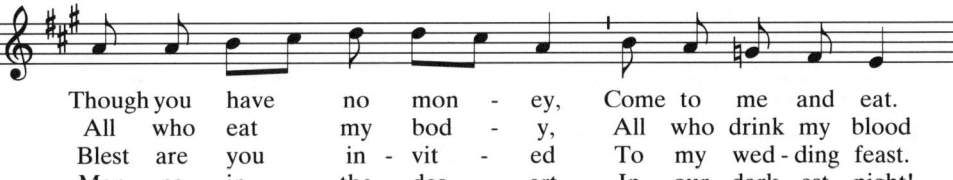

Though you have no mon-ey, Come to me and eat.
All who eat my bod-y, All who drink my blood
Blest are you in-vit-ed To my wed-ding feast.
Man-na in the des-ert, In our dark-est night!

Drink the cup I of-fer; Feed on fin-est wheat!
Shall have joy for-ev-er, Share the life of God.
You shall live for-ev-er, All your joys in-creased.
Food for pil-grim peo-ple, Pledge of glo-ry bright!

5. Many grains become one loaf,
   Many grapes, the wine.
   So shall we one body be,
   Who together dine.
   As the bread is broken,
   As the wine is shared:
   So must we be given,
   Caring as Christ cared.

6. Risen Savior, walk with us,
   Lead us by the hand.
   Heal our blinded eyes and hearts,
   Help us understand.
   Lord, make known your presence
   At this table blest.
   Stay with us forever,
   God, our host and guest!

Text: Delores Dufner, O.S.B. © 1985 Sisters of St. Benedict, St. Joseph, MN 56374
Music: Plainchant, Mode V; acc. Cecile Gertken, O.S.B. © 1989 Sisters of St. Benedict, St. Joseph, MN 56374

ADORO TE
75 75 65 65

35 Let Us Come Before the Lord

REFRAIN

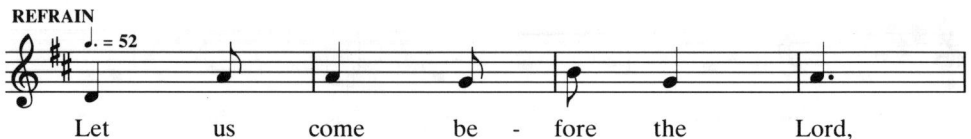
Let us come be - fore the Lord,

sing - ing for joy, prais - ing God's name: to

whom be glo - ry for - ev - er and ev - er!

VERSES

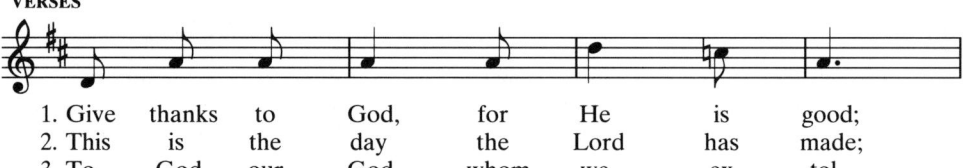
1. Give thanks to God, for He is good;
2. This is the day the Lord has made;
3. To God, our God, whom we ex - tol,

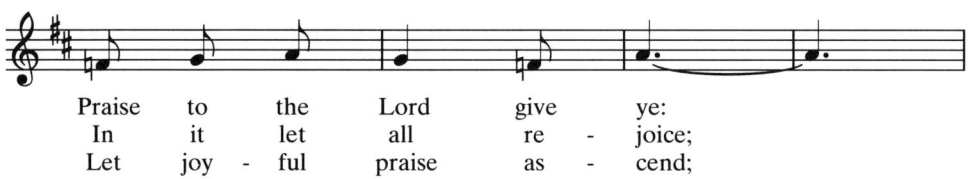
Praise to the Lord give ye:
In it let all re - joice;
Let joy - ful praise as - cend;

Text: Refrain and v. 3: Tobias Colgan, O.S.B. © 1986, 1989 St. Meinrad Archabbey, St. Meinrad, IN 47577; vv. 1, 2: Based on Psalm 118, The Scottish Metrical Psalter, 1650, alt.
Music: Tobias Colgan, O.S.B. © 1986 St. Meinrad Archabbey, St. Meinrad, IN 47577

86 86

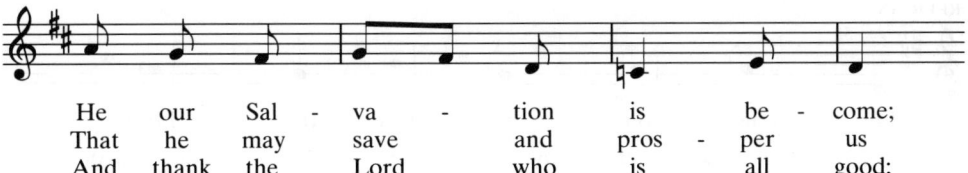

He our Sal - va - tion is be - come;
That he may save and pros - per us
And thank the Lord who is all good;

To Refrain

Our Strength and Song is He.
In pray'r we lift our voice.
Whose mer - cies nev - er end.

36 Libra Mis Ojos de la Muerte

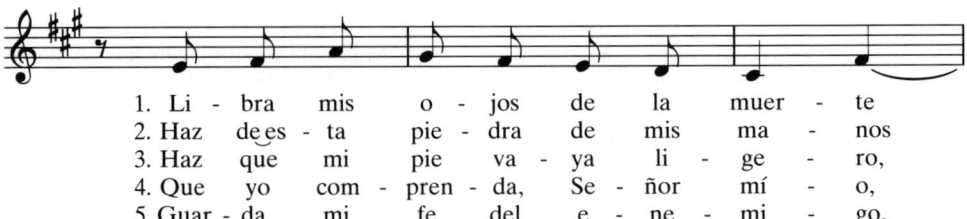

1. Li - bra mis o - jos de la muer - te
2. Haz de es - ta pie - dra de mis ma - nos
3. Haz que mi pie va - ya li - ge - ro,
4. Que yo com - pren - da, Se - ñor mí - o,
5. Guar - da mi fe del e - ne - mi - go,

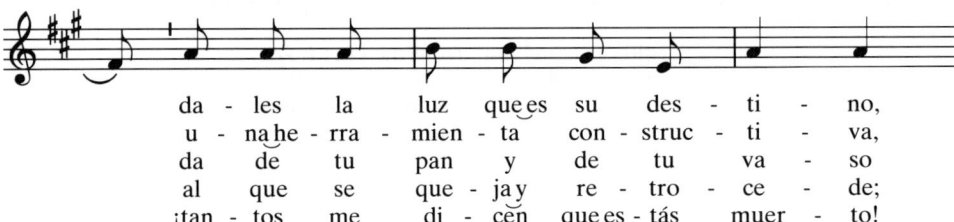

da - les la luz que es su des - ti - no,
u - na he - rra - mien - ta con - struc - ti - va,
da de tu pan y de tu va - so
al que se que - ja y re - tro - ce - de;
¡tan - tos me di - cen que es - tás muer - to!

Yo, co - mo el cie - go del ca - mi - no,
cu - ra su fie - bre po - se - si - va
al que te si - gue pa - so a pa - so
que el co - ra - zón no se me que - de
y en - tre la som - bra y el de - sier - to

pi - do un mi - la - gro pa - ra ver - te.
y á - bre - la al bien de mis her - ma - nos.
por los más du - ro del sen - de - ro.
de - sen - ten - di - da - men - te frí - o.
da - me tu ma - no y ven con - mi - go.

A - men.

Text: © Conferencia Episcopal de Colombia, Secretariado de Liturgia; Non-metrical tr. Tobias Colgan, O.S.B. © 1989 St. Meinrad Archabbey, St. Meinrad, IN 47577
Music: Jesús M. Sasía, O.S.B. © 1987 Abadía Benedictina de San José, Güigüe, Venezuela

1. Free my eyes from death;
   Give them the light for which they
     are destined.
   I, like the blind person on the road,
   Ask for a miracle so I may see you.

2. Make of this stone which is my hands
   A constructive tool;
   Cure its possessive fever
   And open it to the good of my
     brothers and sisters.

3. Make my feet go quickly,
   Give of your bread and your cup
   To the one who follows you step-by-step
   Along the hardest part of the path.

4. May I understand, my Lord,
   Those who complain and turn back;
   May my heart not remain
   Uninterested and cold.

5. Preserve my faith from the enemy,
   So many tell me that you are dead!
   And between the shadow and the desert
   Give me your hand and come with me.

37 Lo! What a Cloud of Witnesses

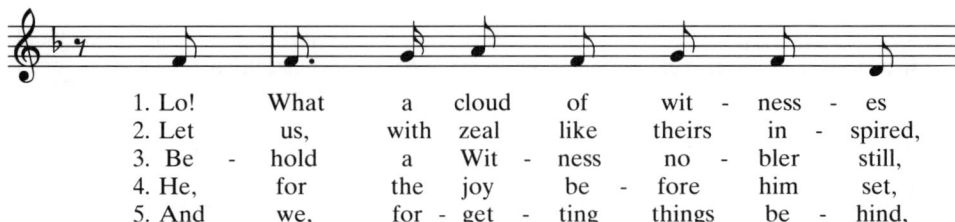

1. Lo! What a cloud of wit-ness-es
2. Let us, with zeal like theirs in-spired,
3. Be-hold a Wit-ness no-bler still,
4. He, for the joy be-fore him set,
5. And we, for-get-ting things be-hind,

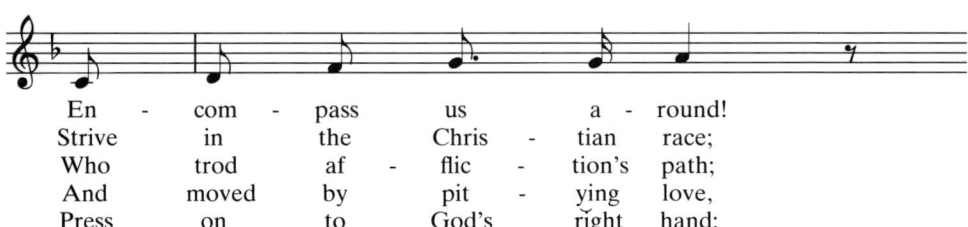

En-com-pass us a-round!
Strive in the Chris-tian race;
Who trod af-flic-tion's path;
And moved by pit-ying love,
Press on to God's right hand;

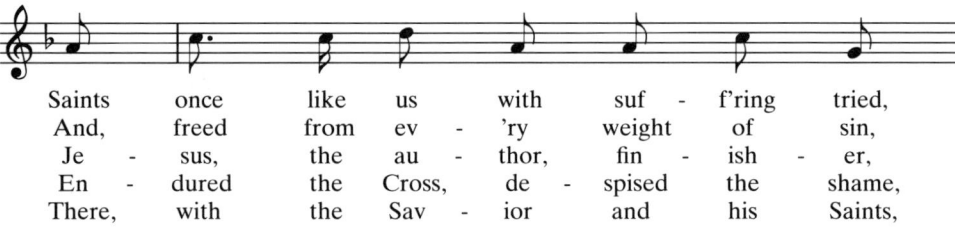

Saints once like us with suf-f'ring tried,
And, freed from ev-'ry weight of sin,
Je-sus, the au-thor, fin-ish-er,
En-dured the Cross, de-spised the shame,
There, with the Sav-ior and his Saints,

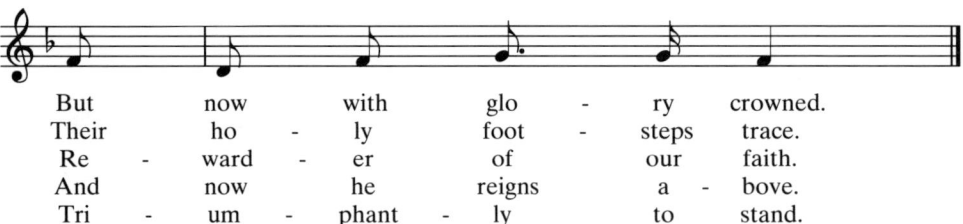

But now with glo-ry crowned.
Their ho-ly foot-steps trace.
Re-ward-er of our faith.
And now he reigns a-bove.
Tri-um-phant-ly to stand.

Text: Translations and Paraphrases, 1745, alt.; para. of Heb. 12:1-3
Music: Robert LeBlanc © 1985 St. Joseph Abbey, St. Benedict, LA 70457

PILGRIM'S PRIZE
86 86

Lord Jesus Christ, Son of David   38

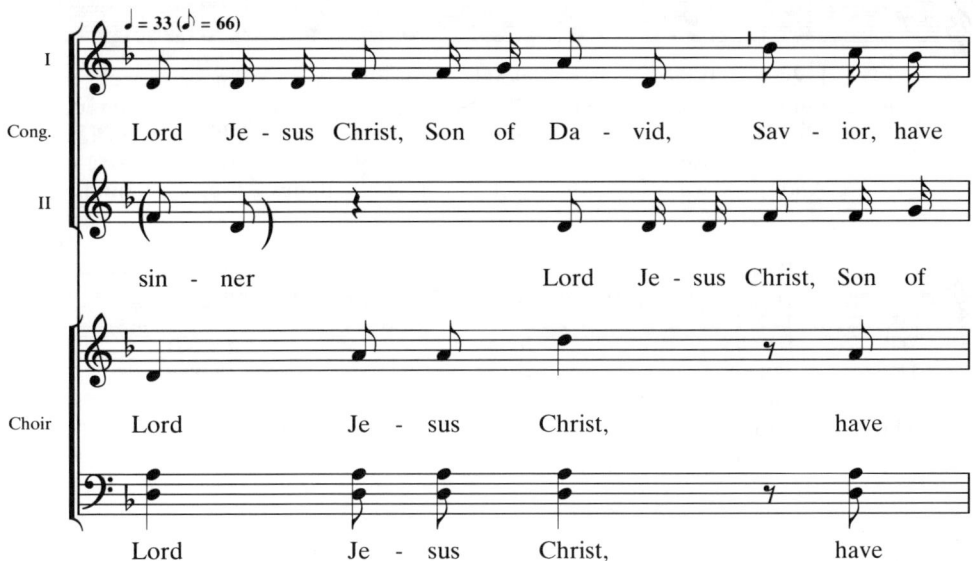

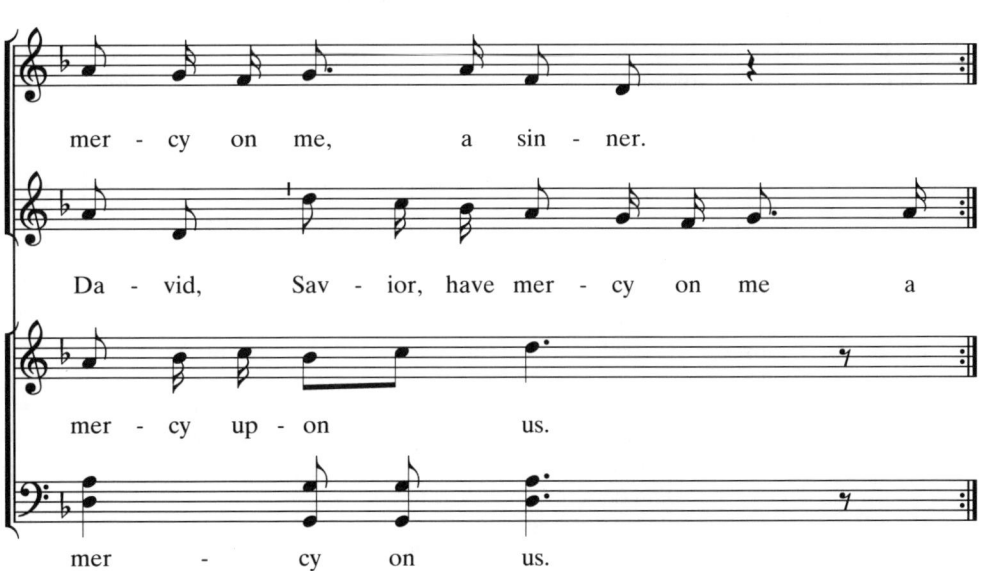

NB 1—Choral parts are optional. Parts may be added individually or together as a choral elaboration to the mantra.
NB 2—As in any mantra, the quality of breathing is important. The proclamation of Christ as Savior requires a
     more vigorous breath, while at the end a slow, measured breath is needed.

Text: *Jesus Prayer*
Music: *Robert LeBlanc © 1984 St. Joseph Abbey, St. Benedict, LA 70457*

39 Lord Jesus, As We Turn from Sin

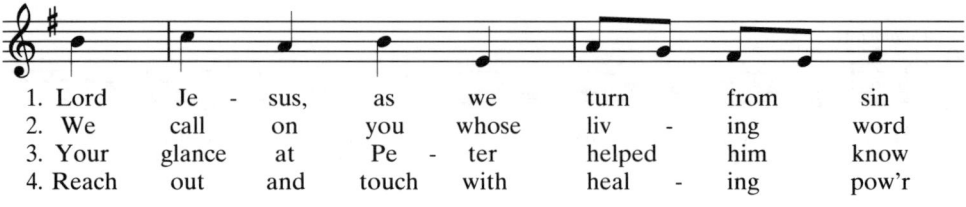

1. Lord Jesus, as we turn from sin
2. We call on you whose living word
3. Your glance at Peter helped him know
4. Reach out and touch with healing pow'r

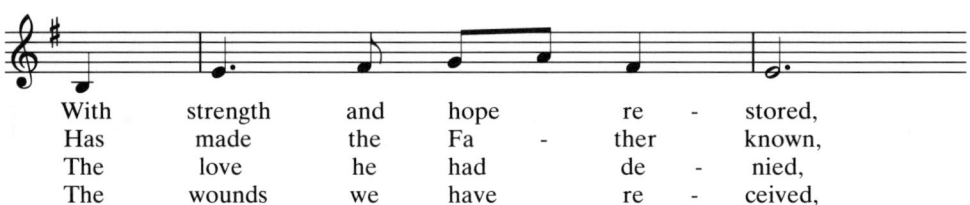

With strength and hope restored,
Has made the Father known,
The love he had denied,
The wounds we have received,

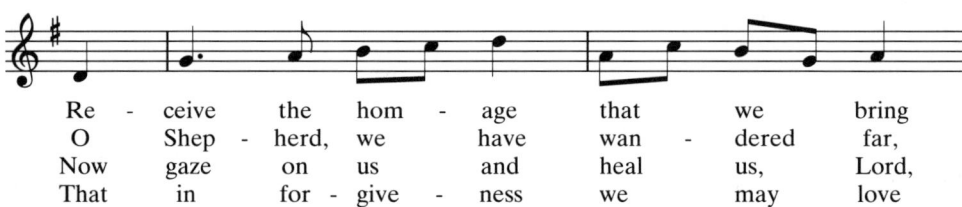

Receive the homage that we bring
O Shepherd, we have wandered far,
Now gaze on us and heal us, Lord,
That in forgiveness we may love

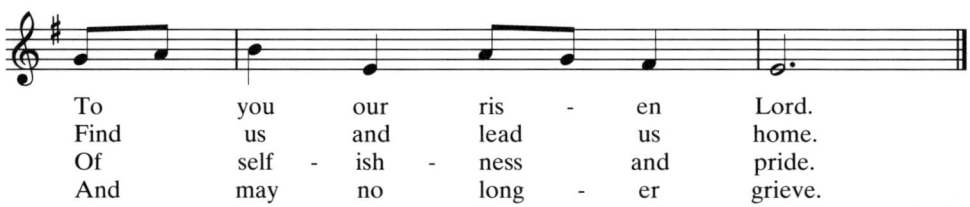

To you our risen Lord.
Find us and lead us home.
Of selfishness and pride.
And may no longer grieve.

5. Then stay with us when ev'ning comes
And darkness makes us blind,
O stay until the light of dawn
May fill both heart and mind.

Text: Ralph Wright, O.S.B. © 1991, ICEL
Music: Tobias Colgan, O.S.B. © 1989 St. Meinrad Archabbey, St. Meinrad, IN 47577

41 Lord, You Are a Banquet

ANTIPHON

Lord, you are a ban-quet for my soul;

you are the joy of my heart, and the praise on my lips.

VERSES

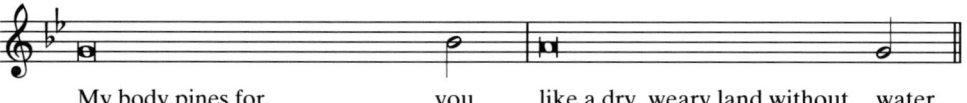

1. O God, you are my God, for you I long; for you my soul is thirsting.
2. So I gaze on you in the sanctuary to see your strength and your glory.
3. So I will bless you all my life; in your name I will lift up my hands.
4. For you have been my help; in the shadow of your wings I re-joice.

My body pines for you like a dry, weary land without water.
For your love is better than life; my lips will speak your praise.
My soul shall be filled as with a banquet; my mouth shall praise you with joy.
My soul clings to you; your right hand holds me fast.

Text: Antiphon: Isaac Borocz, O.S.B. © 1982 St. Anselm's Abbey, Washington, DC 20017; vv. Psalm 63:2–6; 8–9. © 1963–1986 Ladies of the Grail (England). Used by permission of GIA Publications, Inc. Chicago, IL, exclusive agent. All rights reserved.
Music: Isaac Borocz, O.S.B. © 1982 St. Anselm's Abbey, Washington, DC 20017

Merciful Redeemer, Come 42

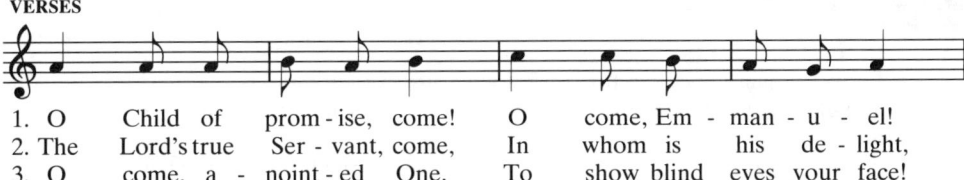

1. O Child of prom-ise, come! O come, Em-man-u-el!
2. The Lord's true Ser-vant, come, In whom is his de-light,
3. O come, a-noint-ed One, To show blind eyes your face!
4. O Man of sor-rows, come, De-spised and cast a-side!

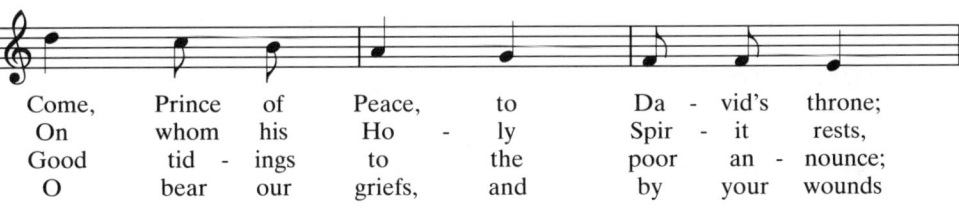

Come, Prince of Peace, to Da-vid's throne;
On whom his Ho-ly Spir-it rests,
Good tid-ings to the poor an-nounce;
O bear our griefs, and by your wounds

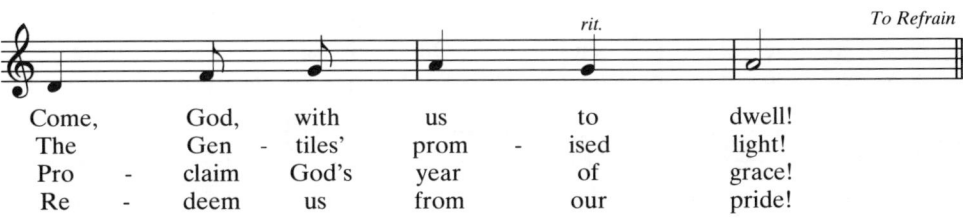

Come, God, with us to dwell!
The Gen-tiles' prom-ised light!
Pro-claim God's year of grace!
Re-deem us from our pride!

5. O come, God's holy Lamb;
   To death be meekly led!
   O save the many by your Blood,
   For sin so gladly shed!

6. O come, Messiah King,
   To reign in endless light,
   When heav'nly peace at last goes forth
   From Sion's holy height!

Text: Refrain: Tobias Colgan, O.S.B. © 1986 St. Meinrad Archabbey, St. Meinrad, IN 47577; vv. 1969 James Quinn, S.J., Reprinted by permission of Geoffrey Chapman, a division of Cassell Publishers Limited.
Music: Tobias Colgan, O.S.B. © 1986 St. Meinrad Archabbey, St. Meinrad, IN 47577

43 Not in the Wind

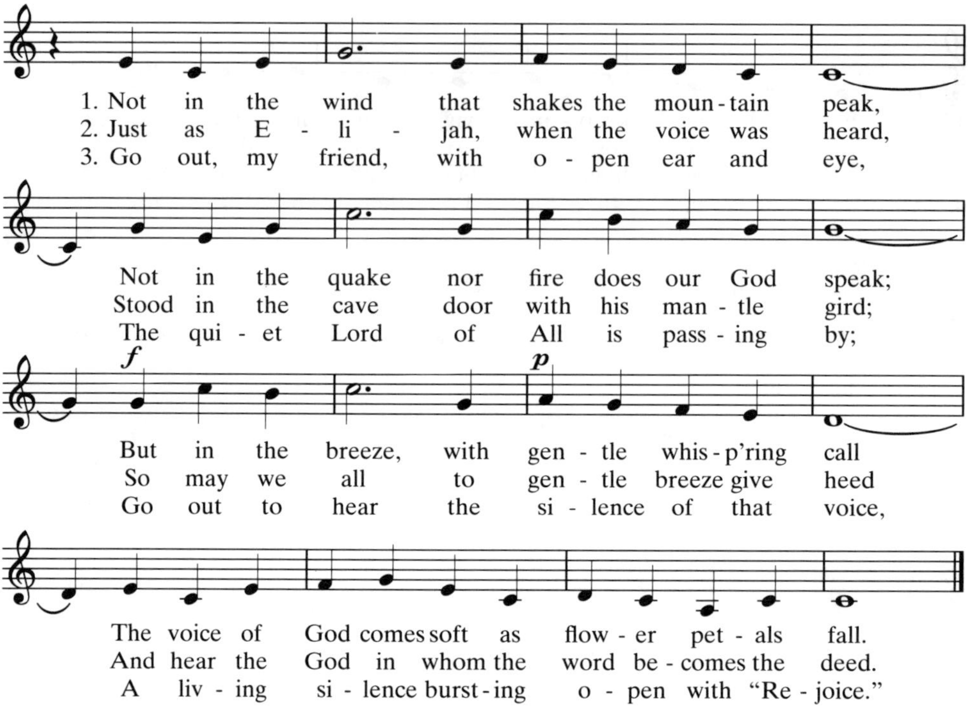

1. Not in the wind that shakes the moun-tain peak,
   Not in the quake nor fire does our God speak;
   But in the breeze, with gen-tle whis-p'ring call
   The voice of God comes soft as flow-er pet-als fall.
2. Just as E-li-jah, when the voice was heard,
   Stood in the cave door with his man-tle gird;
   So may we all to gen-tle breeze give heed
   And hear the God in whom the word be-comes the deed.
3. Go out, my friend, with o-pen ear and eye,
   The qui-et Lord of All is pass-ing by;
   Go out to hear the si-lence of that voice,
   A liv-ing si-lence burst-ing o-pen with "Re-joice."

Text: Based on 1 Kings 19:9–14. Jane Klimisch, O.S.B. © 1984 Sacred Heart Convent, Yankton, SD 57078
Music: Jane Klimisch, O.S.B. © 1984 Sacred Heart Convent, Yankton, SD 57078

THE GENTLE BREEZE
10 10 D

44 Now Go, the Mass Is Ended

1. "Now go, the Mass is end-ed;" Our mis-sion we pro-claim:
   To live in peace and jus-tice, To praise God's ho-ly name;
   To feed the poor and hun-gry, To care for those in need,
   To wor-ship and to la-bor, To love in word and deed.
2. "Now go, the Mass is end-ed;" With hope our hearts are filled;
   To-geth-er as one fam-'ly The king-dom we shall build:
   A world of peace and free-dom, Of love and har-mo-ny,
   "Do this in sa-cred mem-'ry, In mem-o-ry of Me!"

Text: Jane Klimisch, O.S.B. © 1989 Sacred Heart Convent, Yankton, SD 57078

AURELIA
76 76 D

Now We Gather, Keeping Vigil 45

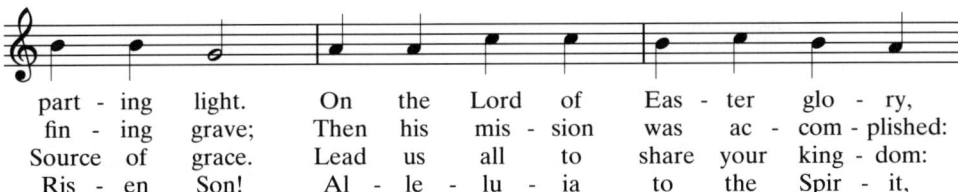

1. Now we gather, keeping vigil in the fast de-
2. Night when Christ arose victorious from death's dark con-
3. Stay with us we humbly beg you, risen Savior,
4. Alleluia to the Father, and to Christ, his

parting light. On the Lord of Easter glory,
fining grave; Then his mission was accomplished:
Source of grace. Lead us all to share your kingdom:
Risen Son! Alleluia to the Spirit,

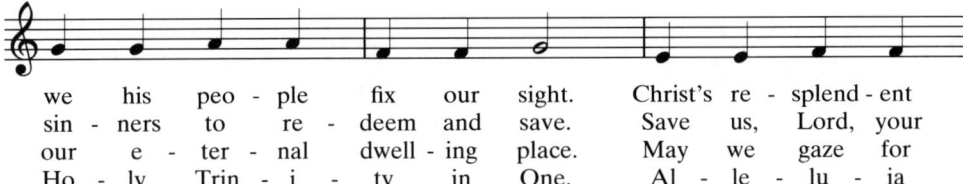

we his people fix our sight. Christ's resplendent
sinners to redeem and save. Save us, Lord, your
our eternal dwelling place. May we gaze for
Holy Trinity in One. Alleluia

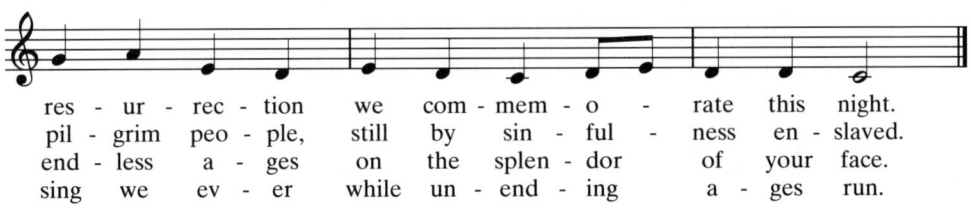

resurrection we commemorate this night.
pilgrim people, still by sinfulness enslaved.
endless ages on the splendor of your face.
sing we ever while unending ages run.

Text: Matthew Leavy, O.S.B. © 1986 St. Anselm Abbey, Manchester, NH 03102
Music: Henry Bryan Hays, O.S.B. © 1981 Order of St. Benedict, Collegeville, MN 56321

SUN JOURNEY
87 87 87

46 O Come, Bless the Lord

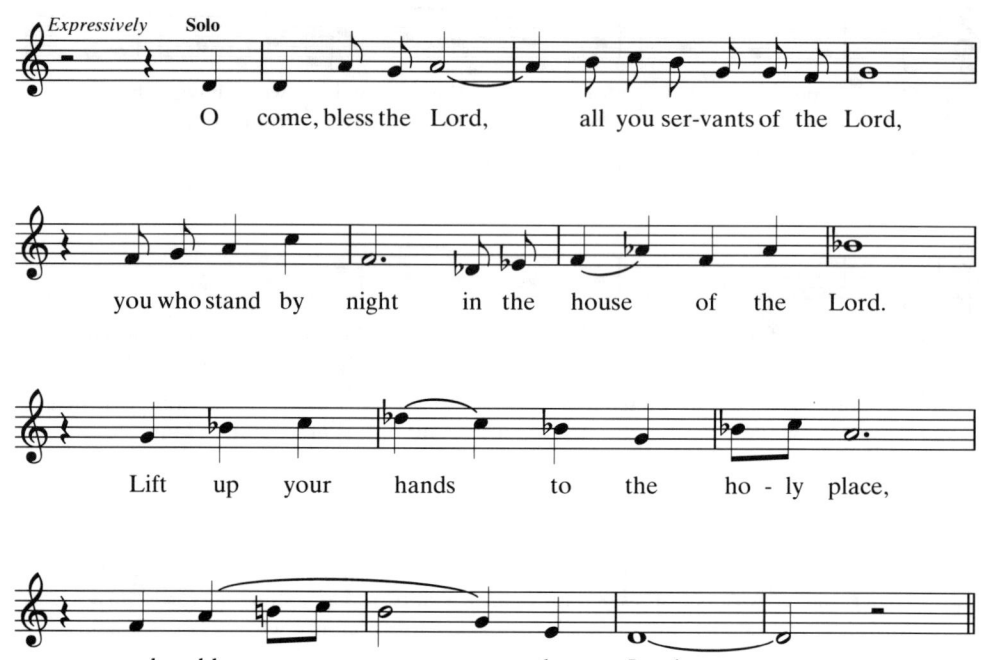

Text: Psalm 134, alt. Aelred Kavanagh, O.S.B. © 1989 St. Joseph Abbey, St. Benedict, LA 70457
Music: Sean Duggan, O.S.B. © 1989 St. Joseph Abbey, St. Benedict, LA 70457

47. O Come, Let Us Follow

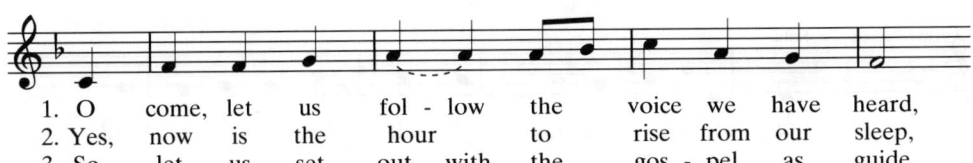

1. O come, let us fol - low the voice we have heard,
2. Yes, now is the hour to rise from our sleep,
3. So let us set out with the gos - pel as guide,

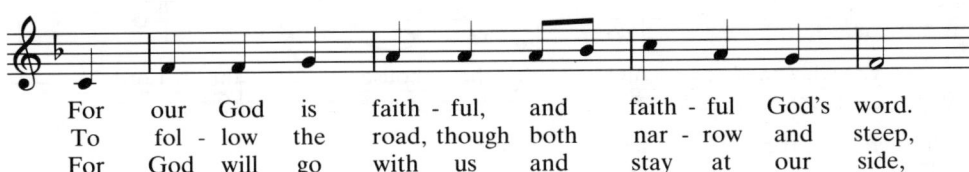

For our God is faith - ful, and faith - ful God's word.
To fol - low the road, though both nar - row and steep,
For God will go with us and stay at our side,

As pil - grims we jour - ney by faith through the night,
To leave works of dark - ness and has - ten towards day,
And love shall im - pel us to climb ev - 'ry height,

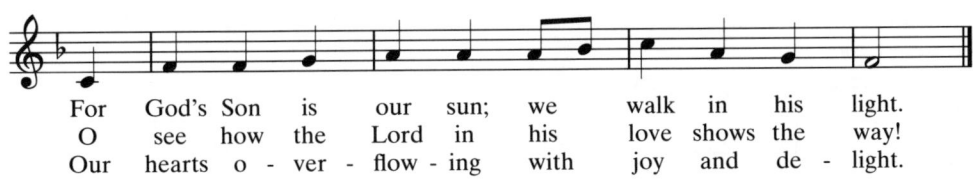

For God's Son is our sun; we walk in his light.
O see how the Lord in his love shows the way!
Our hearts o - ver - flow - ing with joy and de - light.

Text: Delores Dufner, O.S.B. © 1987 Sisters of St. Benedict, St. Joseph, MN 56374

MARIA ZU LIEBEN
11 11 D

48 O Father, Lead Us Back to You

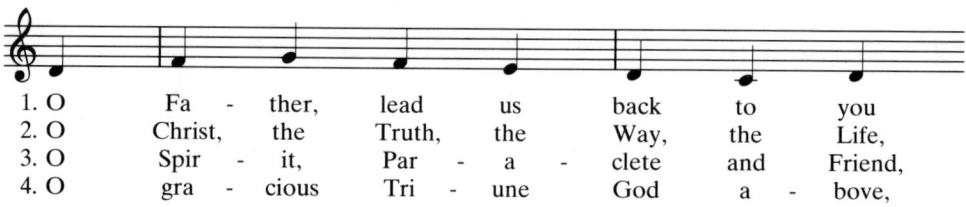

1. O Father, lead us back to you
2. O Christ, the Truth, the Way, the Life,
3. O Spirit, Paraclete and Friend,
4. O gracious Triune God above,

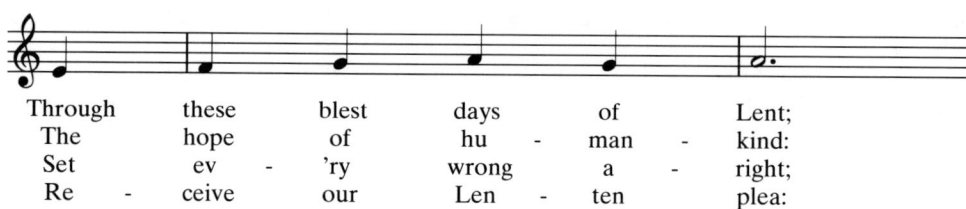

Through these blest days of Lent;
The hope of humankind:
Set ev-'ry wrong aright;
Receive our Lenten plea:

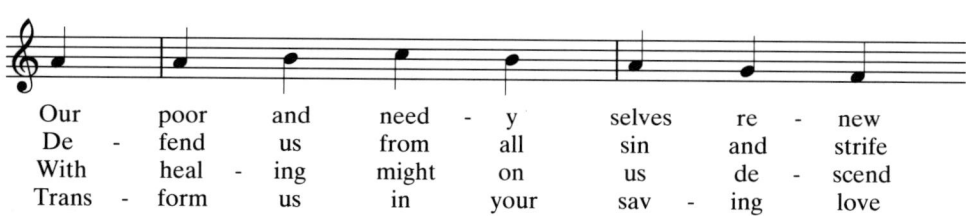

Our poor and needy selves renew
Defend us from all sin and strife
With healing might on us descend
Transform us in your saving love

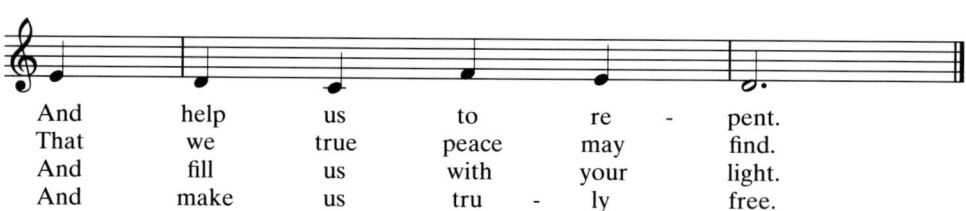

And help us to repent.
That we true peace may find.
And fill us with your light.
And make us truly free.

Text: Becket Gerald Senchur, O.S.B. © 1983 St. Vincent Archabbey, Latrobe, PA 15650
Music: Becket Gerald Senchur, O.S.B. © 1983 St. Vincent Archabbey, Latrobe, PA 15650

O Let All That Has Life 49
Verses for three equal voices

Text: Delores Dufner, O.S.B. © 1985 Sisters of St. Benedict, St. Joseph, MN 56374
Music: Robert LeBlanc © 1985 Sisters of St. Benedict, St. Joseph, MN 56374

VERSE 5

Oh Bondadoso Creador, Escucha 50

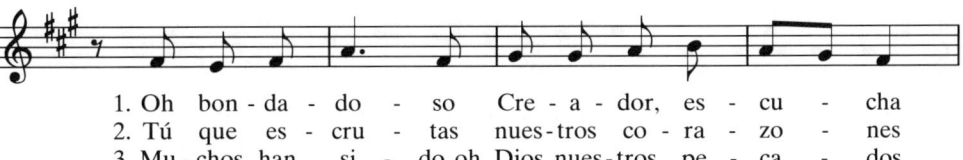

1. Oh bon-da-do-so Cre-a-dor, es-cu-cha
2. Tú que es-cru-tas nues-tros co-ra-zo-nes
3. Mu-chos han si-do, oh Dios, nues-tros pe-ca-dos,
4. En es-te tiem-po an-de-mos vi-gi-lan-tes,

nues-tra voz, nues-tras sú-pli-cas hu-mil-des
y co-no-ces de qué fui-mos cre-a-dos,
con do-lor an-te Ti los con-fe-sa-mos;
en a-yu-no, o-ra-ción y bue-nas o-bras,

que en es-te san-to tiem-po de Cua-res-ma
con-ce-de tu per-dón y tu in-dul-gen-cia
nues-tra con-fian-za es-tá só-lo en tu Nom-bre
y en su Pa-la-bra es-pe-re nues-tra al-ma

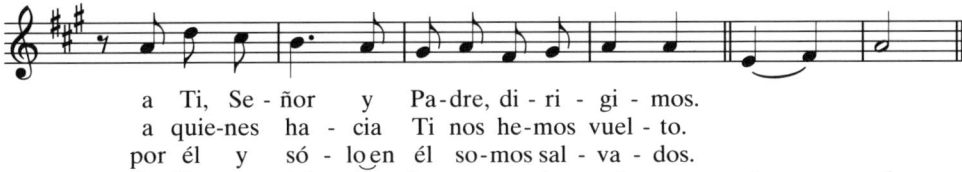

a Ti, Se-ñor y Pa-dre, di-ri-gi-mos.
a quie-nes ha-cia Ti nos he-mos vuel-to.
por él y só-lo en él so-mos sal-va-dos.
la Pas-cua del Se-ñor con a-le-grí-a. A-mén.

1. Oh kindly Creator, listen to our voice,
   to our humble petitions,
   which in this holy time of Lent
   we address to you, Lord and Father.

2. You who examine our hearts
   and know of what we were made,
   grant your forgiveness and indulgence
   to us who have turned toward you.

3. Our sins have been many, O God;
   with sorrow we confess them before you.
   Our confidence is in your name alone;
   by it and only in it are we saved.

4. In this time let us walk vigilantly,
   in fasting, prayer and good works,
   and in your Word may our soul await
   the Pasch of the Lord with joy.

Text: © Monasterio Benedictino de las Condes, Santiago, Chile; Non-metrical tr.: Tobias Colgan, O.S.B. © 1989 St. Meinrad Archabbey, St. Meinrad, IN 47577
Music: León Tolosa, O.S.B. © 1987 Monasterio Benedictino de las Condes, Santiago, Chile; acc.: Jesús M. Sasía, O.S.B. © 1989 Abadía Benedictina de San José, Güigüe, Venezuela

51 On Our Journey to the Kingdom

1. On our jour-ney to the king-dom For-ward goes our pil-grim band,
2. One the light of God's own pres-ence On this ran-somed peo-ple shed,
3. One the song that lips of thou-sands Lift as from the heart of one;

Sing-ing songs of ex-pec-ta-tion, March-ing to the prom-ised land.
Chas-ing far all gloom and ter-ror, Bright'-ning all the path we tread.
One the con-flict, one the per-il, One the march in Christ be-gun.

Clear be-fore us through the dark-ness Gleams and burns the guid-ing light;
One the ob-ject of our jour-ney, One the faith which nev-er tires,
One the glad-ness of re-joic-ing On the far e-ter-nal shore,

Pil-grim clasps the hand of pil-grim, Step-ping fear-less through the night.
One the ear-nest look-ing for-ward, One the hope our God in-spires.
Where the one al-might-y Fath-er Reigns in love for-ev-er-more.

Text: Bernhardt S. Ingemann, 1789–1862. tr. S. Baring-Gould, alt.
Music: Tobias Colgan, O.S.B. © 1983 St. Meinrad Archabbey, St. Meinrad, IN 47577

52 Out of Everlasting Stillness

1. Out of ev-er-last-ing still-ness run the wa-ters of the flood;
2. We are car-ried to the Fa-ther on this sac-ra-men-tal tide,
3. And it feeds the heal-ing branch-es and the leaves that nev-er fade
4. To the Fa-ther, Son, and Spir-it, songs of grate-ful wor-ship sing.

Out of springs with-out be-gin-ning flow the wa-ter and the blood.
On the ri-ver of the Spir-it from the Sav-ior's o-pen side.
On the trees of life that flow-er where the tree of death was raised.
God of nur-ture and of new-ness, hear the praise your peo-ple bring.

Text: Miriam Pollard, O.C.S.O. © 1985 Mount St. Mary's Abbey, Wrentham, MA 02093
Music: Edith Scholl, O.C.S.O. © 1985 Mount St. Mary's Abbey, Wrentham, MA 02093

Oye Nuestra Voz, Oh Cristo 53

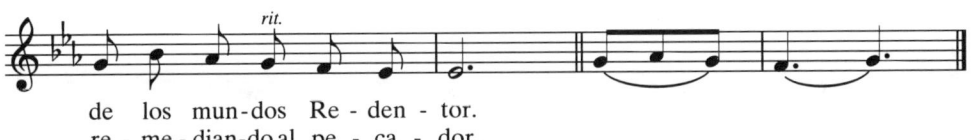

1. O - ye nues-tra voz, oh Cris - to, de los cie-los Cre - a - dor,
2. La muer-te que a-rruí-na al or - be con - mo-vió tu co - ra - zón,
3. En la ple - ni - tud del tiem - po, cual de tá - la - mo nup - cial,
4. To - dos te rin - den tri - bu - tos y hon-ran tu gran ma - jes - tad;
5. Con fe vi - va te pe - di - mos, jus - to juez u - ni - ver - sal,
6. A ti, Cris - to, rey cle - men - te, a ti, Pa - dre cre - a - dor,

luz e - ter - na de los fie - les,
y sal - vas - te al mun - do en - fer - mo
sa - lis - te del cas - to se - no
to - dos los se - res te a - cla - man:
nos li - bres en to - do tiem - po
con el Es - pí - ri - tu San - to

rit.

de los mun - dos Re - den - tor.
re - me - dian-do al pe - ca - dor.
de la Ma - dre vir - gi - nal.
la tie - rra, el cie - lo y el mar.
de los dar - dos de Sa - tán.
se tri - bu - te siem-pre ho-nor. A - mén.

1. Hear our voice, O Christ,
   Creator of the heavens,
   light eternal of the faithful,
   Redeemer of the worlds.

2. The death that ruins the world
   moved your heart,
   and you saved the sick world,
   saving the sinner.

3. In the fullness of time,
   just as from the marriage bed,
   you came forth from the chaste womb
   of the virgin Mother.

4. All render tribute to you
   and honor your great majesty;
   all beings acclaim you:
   the earth, the sky and the sea.

5. With lively faith we implore you,
   just and universal judge,
   to free us at all times
   from the darts of Satan.

6. To you, Christ, merciful king,
   to you, Father creator,
   with the Holy Spirit
   may honor always be paid.

Text: © Conferencia Episcopal de Colombia, Secretariado de Liturgia; Non-metrical tr. Tobias Colgan, O.S.B. © 1989 St. Meinrad Archabbey, St. Meinrad, IN 47577
Music: Jesús M. Sasía, O.S.B. © 1987 Abadía Benedictina de San José, Güigüe, Venezuela

54 Renewed in Your Great Love

REFRAIN

Renewed in your great love, God, our Creator,

we stand to praise and bless your name.

VERSES

1. Christ Jesus, Savior, stands before your presence
2. Relying on your providential care for us,
3. We want to see you in the people near us;

as intercessor knowing well our frailty.
we call now to mind all the gifts and graces
we want to hear you speaking in our world today.

We seek your mercy, confident you hear us.
you show'r upon us in your great compassion.
Help us be open to your word within our lives.

Text: Monika Ellis, O.S.B. © 1989 St. Placid Priory, Lacey, WA 98506
Music: Plainchant, Mode V; acc. Cecile Gertken, O.S.B. © 1989 Sisters of St. Benedict, St. Joseph, MN 56374

ATTENDE DOMINE
11 11 11 with refrain

Savior of the Nations, Come 55

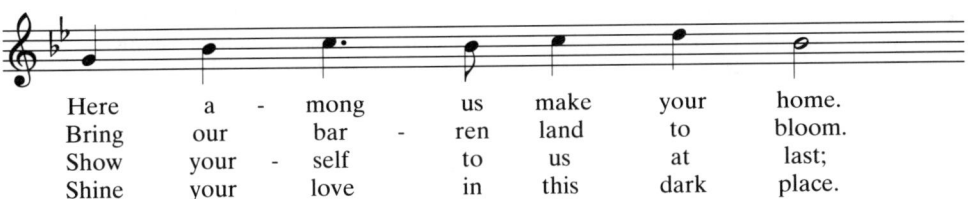

1. Sa - vior of the na - tions, come;
2. Dew from heav - en, gent - ly come;
3. Long - de - sired of a - ges past,
4. Ra - diance of God's ho - ly face,

Here a - mong us make your home.
Bring our bar - ren land to bloom.
Show your - self to us at last;
Shine your love in this dark place.

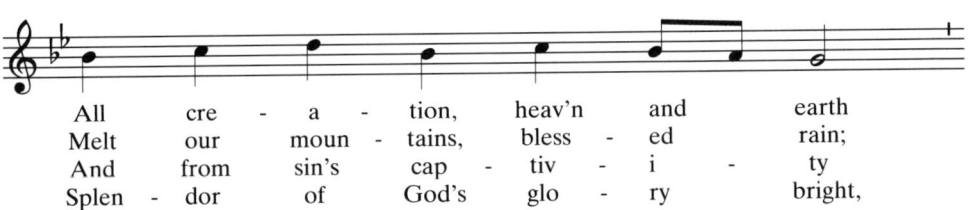

All cre - a - tion, heav'n and earth
Melt our moun - tains, bless - ed rain;
And from sin's cap - tiv - i - ty
Splen - dor of God's glo - ry bright,

Groan un - til you come to birth.
Let proud hills be lev - el plain.
Call us back and set us free.
Lead us to e - ter - nal light!

Text: Delores Dufner, O.S.B. © 1983 Sisters of St. Benedict, St. Joseph, MN 56374
Music: J. Walther, Geistliche Gesangbüchlein, 1524; acc. © 1984 Jay F. Hunstiger, 4545 Wichita Trail, Medina, MN 55340

NUN KOMM DER HEIDEN HEILAND
77 77

56 Sing of Glory and His Body*

1. Sing of glory and his body, Wondrous
2. Gift for us and gift forever, From the
3. At the last, the paschal supper, With his
4. Word made flesh by word made present Body

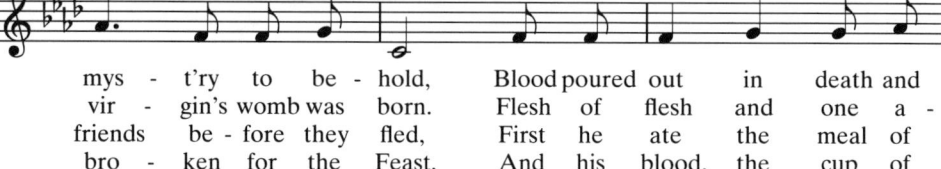

myst'ry to behold, Blood poured out in death and
virgin's womb was born. Flesh of flesh and one a-
friends before they fled, First he ate the meal of
broken for the Feast, And his blood, the cup of

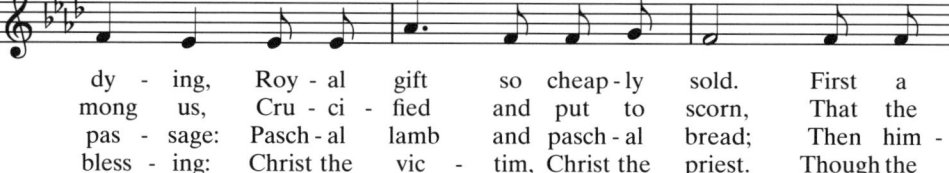

dying, Royal gift so cheaply sold. First a
mong us, Crucified and put to scorn, That the
passage: Paschal lamb and paschal bread; Then him-
blessing: Christ the victim, Christ the priest. Though the

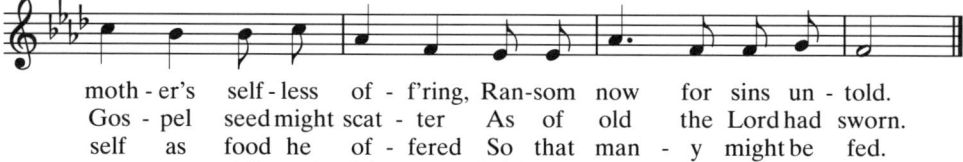

mother's selfless off'ring, Ransom now for sins untold.
Gospel seed might scatter As of old the Lord had sworn.
self as food he offered So that many might be fed.
senses fail and falter, Faith confirms true hearts in peace.

5. Holy sacrament most holy,
   Let us bow on bended knee;
   Visions of the ancient promise
   Now fulfilled in mystery.
   Faith declares what none dare fathom;
   Faith reveals what none may see.

6. To Begetter and Begotten
   Triumph, praise, and majesty,
   Honor, glory, and salvation,
   Blessing for eternity,
   With the one proceeding always,
   Equally in unity.

* May be sung to PANGE LINGUA melody

Text: Harry Hagan, O.S.B. © 1989 St. Meinrad Archabbey, St. Meinrad, IN 47577
Music: Robert LeBlanc © 1980 St. Joseph Abbey, St. Benedict, LA 70457

ST. ANDREW
87 87 87

Sing We of the Blessed Mother   57

1. Sing we of the bless-ed Moth-er Who re-ceived the an - gel's word,
2. Sing we, too, of Mar-y's sor - rows, Of the sword that pierced her through,
3. Sing a - gain the joys of Mar - y When she saw the ris - en Lord,
4. Sing the great-est joy of Mar - y When on earth her work was done,

And o - be - dient to the sum-mons Bore in love the in - fant Lord;
When be-neath the cross of Je - sus She his weight of suf - f'ring knew,
And in pray'r with Christ's a - pos - tles, Wait - ed on his prom-ised word:
And the Lord of all cre - a - tion Brought her to his heav'n-ly home:

Sing we of the joys of Mar - y At whose breast that child was fed
Looked up - on her Son and Sav - ior Reign-ing from the aw - ful tree,
From on high the blaz-ing glo - ry Of the Spir - it's pres - ence came,
Vir - gin Moth-er, Mar - y bless-ed, Raised on high and crowned with grace,

Who is Son of God e - ter - nal And the ev - er - last-ing Bread.
Saw the price of our Re-demp-tion Paid to set the sin - ner free.
Heav'n-ly breath of God's own be - ing, To - kened in the wind and flame.
May your Son, the world's re - deem - er, Grant us all to see his face.

Text: George B. Timms, from English Praise 1975 by permission of Oxford University Press.
Music: Robert LeBlanc © 1983 St. Joseph Abbey, St. Benedict, LA 70457

RAMPARTS
87 87 D

58 Sing, Sing Praise to Creator God

1. Sing, sing praise to Cre-a-tor God, To the God who reigns a-bove.
2. Sing, sing praise to Re-deem-er God, To the Lord who rose on high.
3. Sing, sing praise to the Spir-it God, To the Spir-it who is Light.
4. Sing, sing praise to the Tri-une God, To the One who reigns a-bove.

Hail the Lord who is ev-er a-dored, For we are made in love.
Hail the Lord who is ev-er a-dored, For we shall nev-er die.
Hail the Lord who is ev-er a-dored, For we are led a-right.
Hail the Lord who is ev-er a-dored, For we shall live in love.

To the end of the world From be-gin-ning of time
To the dark of the night From the break of the day
To the depths of the sea From the stars of the sky
To the chill breeze of Fall From the warm breath of Spring

Let the whole of cre-a-tion chime:
Let the whole of cre-a-tion say:
Let the whole of cre-a-tion cry:
Let the whole of cre-a-tion sing:

"May the name of God be praised Both

1.–3. now and for ev-er."
4. now and for ev-er."

Text: Gary Poole and Aelred Rosser, O.S.B. © 1986 Conception Abbey, Conception, MO 64433
Music: Timothy Schoen, O.S.B. © 1986 Conception Abbey, Conception, MO 64433

60 Take Courage, Have Faith

ANTIPHON

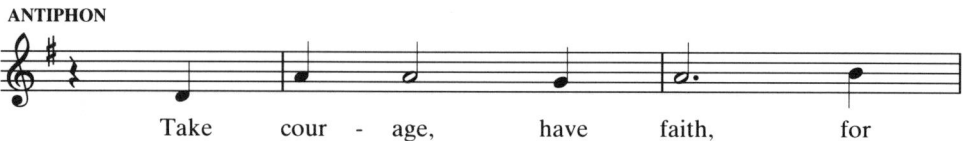

Take cour - age, have faith, for

I have ov - er - come the world, Al - le - lu - ia!

VERSES

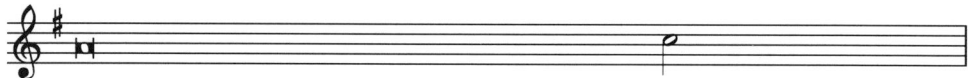

1. I will extol you, O Lord, for you have drawn me up,
2. Sing praises to the Lord, O you saints,
3. You have turned my mourning into dancing;

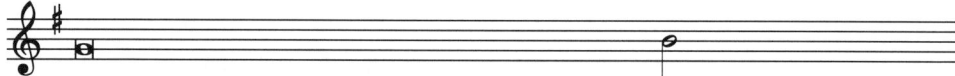

and have not let my foes rejoice over me.
and give thanks to God's holy name.
You have loosened my sackcloth and girded me with gladness,

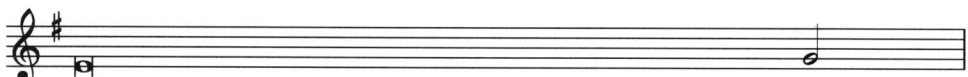

O Lord, you have brought up my soul from She - ol,
For God's anger is but for a moment, and the Lord's favor is for a lifetime.
that my soul may praise you and not be silent.

restored me to life from among those gone down to the Pit.
Weeping may tarry for the night, but joy comes with the morning.
O Lord my God, I will give thanks to you for - ever.

Text: Antiphon: Isaac Borocz, O.S.B. © 1988 St. Anselm's Abbey, Washington, DC 20017; vv. Psalm 30: 2, 4, 5, 6, 12, 13 from the Revised Standard Version of the Bible © 1946, 1952, 1971 by the Division of Christian Education of the National Council of Churches of Christ in the USA and used by permission. All rights reserved.
Music: Isaac Borocz, O.S.B. © 1988 St. Anselm's Abbey, Washington, DC 20017

Take courage, have faith, for **I have overcome** the world.

ALLELUIA!

61 Teach Me the Way of Your Decrees

ANTIPHON

Teach me the way of your de-crees, O Lord.

VERSE 1

In-struct me, O Lord, in the way of your stat-utes, that I may ex-

act-ly ob-serve them. Give me dis-cern-ment, that

To Antiphon

I may ob-serve your law and keep it with all my heart.

VERSE 2

Lead me in the path of your com-mands, for in it I de-light.

To Antiphon

In-cline my heart to your de-crees and not to gain.

Text: Psalm 119: 33–37; 40 © *New American Bible*, 1970 Confraternity of Christian Doctrine, Washington, DC 20017
Music: Sean Duggan, O.S.B. © 1988 St. Joseph Abbey, St. Benedict, LA 70457

VERSE 3

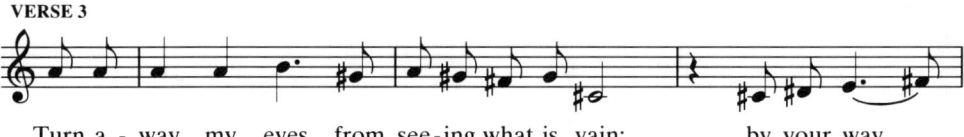

Turn a-way my eyes from see-ing what is vain: by your way

give me life. Be-hold, I long for your pre-cepts;

To Antiphon

in your jus - tice give me life.

The Blazing Sun Has Run Its Course 62

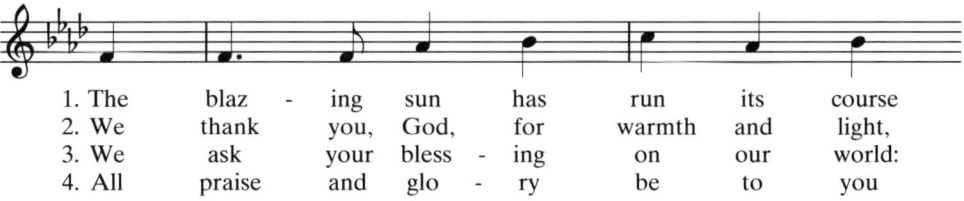

1. The blaz - ing sun has run its course
2. We thank you, God, for warmth and light,
3. We ask your bless - ing on our world:
4. All praise and glo - ry be to you

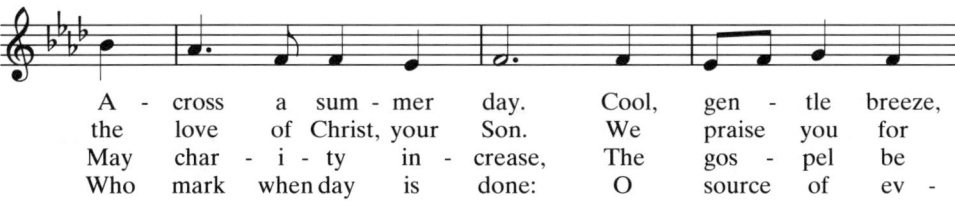

A - cross a sum - mer day. Cool, gen - tle breeze,
the love of Christ, your Son. We praise you for
May char - i - ty in - crease, The gos - pel be
Who mark when day is done: O source of ev -

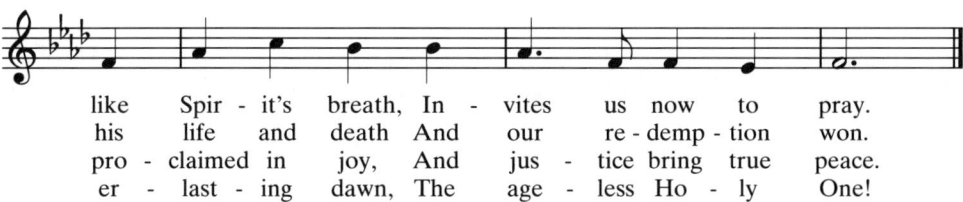

like Spir - it's breath, In - vites us now to pray.
his life and death And our re - demp - tion won.
pro - claimed in joy, And jus - tice bring true peace.
er - last - ing dawn, The age - less Ho - ly One!

Text: Delores Dufner, O.S.B. © 1985 Sisters of St. Benedict, St. Joseph, MN 56374
Music: © 1985 Jay F. Hunstiger, 4545 Wichita Trail, Medina, MN 55340

63 The Cup of Salvation

REFRAIN

The cup of sal-va-tion I will take up.

I will call up-on the Lord's name, and

of-fer a sac-ri-fice of thanks to God.

VERSE 1

How can I re-pay the Lord for such good-ness to

me? The cup of sal-va-tion I will take up;

To Refrain

I will call on the Lord's name.

Text: Refrain: Tobias Colgan, O.S.B. © 1986 St. Meinrad Archabbey, St. Meinrad, IN 47577. Psalm 116:12–13; 16–19, alt. © 1963–1986 Ladies of the Grail (England). Used by permission of GIA Publications, Inc., Chicago, IL, exclusive agent. All rights reserved.
Music: Tobias Colgan, O.S.B. © 1986 St. Meinrad Archabbey, St. Meinrad, IN 47577

VERSE 2

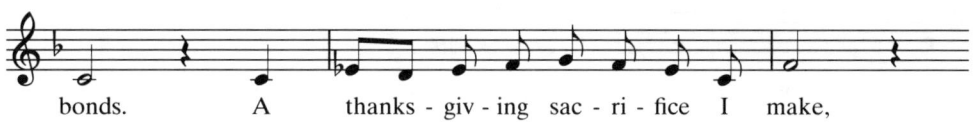

VERSE 3

64 The Lord Is Kind and Merciful

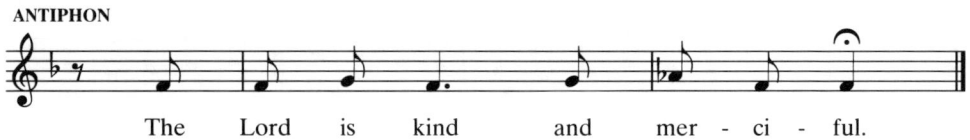

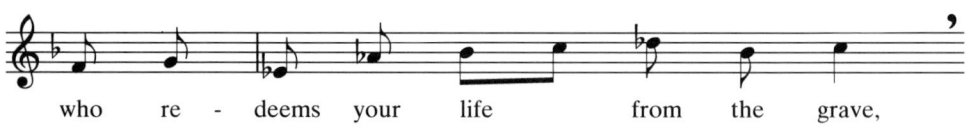

Text: English translation of the refrain from the *Lectionary for Mass* © 1969 ICEL. Vv. Psalm 103: 1–4; 8–11 alt. © 1963–1986 Ladies of the Grail (England). Used by permission of GIA Publications, Inc., Chicago, IL, exclusive agent. All rights reserved.
Music: Robert LeBlanc © 1984 St. Joseph Abbey, St. Benedict, LA 70457

VERSE 3

VERSE 4

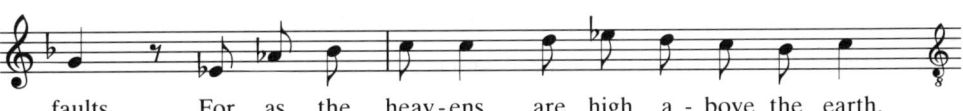

SSA or TTB

65 The Lord Said to My Lord

ANTIPHON

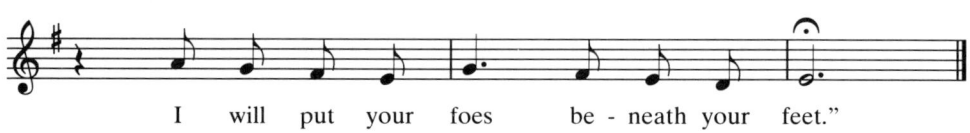

VERSE 1

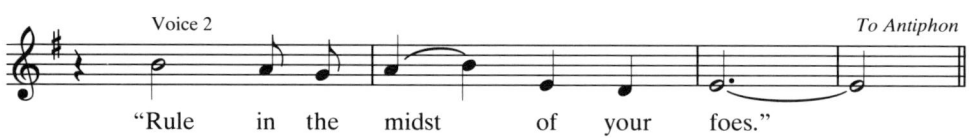

VERSE 2

Text: Psalm 110: 1–5; 7 alt. © 1988 Aelred Kavanagh, O.S.B., St. Joseph Abbey, St. Benedict, LA 70457
Music: Sean Duggan, O.S.B. © 1988 St. Joseph Abbey, St. Benedict, LA 70457

There Is No Greater Love 66

ANTIPHON

There is no great-er love than this: to lay down one's life for one's friends.

VERSES

1. I will give thanks to you Lord, with my whole   heart;
2. When my enemies turned   back,
3. But the Lord sits enthroned for   ever:
4. You, Lord, are a stronghold in time of   trouble,
5. Sing praises to the Lord, who dwells in   Zion!

I will tell of all your wonderful   deeds.
they stumbled and perished be - fore you.
The Lord has established his throne for   judgment;
And those who know your name put their trust in   you,
Tell among the peoples God's   deeds!

I will be glad and exult in   you,
For you have maintained my just   cause;
Judging the world with   righteousness,

For the needy shall not always be for - gotten,

To Antiphon

I will sing praise to your name, O Most   High.
you have sat on the throne giving righteous   judgment.
Judging the people with   equity.
for you have not forsaken those who   seek you.
and the hope of the poor shall not perish for - ever.

Text: Antiphon: Isaac Borocz, O.S.B. © 1982 St. Anselm's Abbey, Washington, DC 20017; vv. Psalm 9:2–5; 8–12; 19 from the Revised Standard Version of the Bible © 1946, 1952, 1971 by the Division of Christian Education of the National Council of Churches of Christ in the USA and used by permission. All rights reserved.
Music: Isaac Borocz, O.S.B. © 1982 St. Anselm's Abbey, Washington, DC 20017

67 The Word of God

1. The Word of God is source and seed;
2. The Word of God is breath and life;
3. The Word of God is flesh and grace

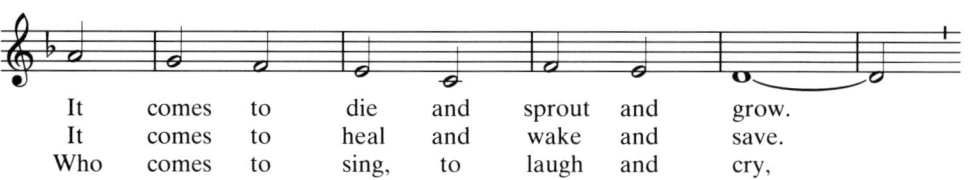

It comes to die and sprout and grow.
It comes to heal and wake and save.
Who comes to sing, to laugh and cry,

So make your dark earth wel - come - warm;
So let the Spir - it touch and mend
So dare to be as once he was,

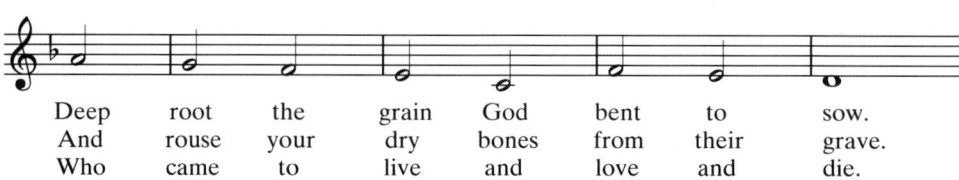

Deep root the grain God bent to sow.
And rouse your dry bones from their grave.
Who came to live and love and die.

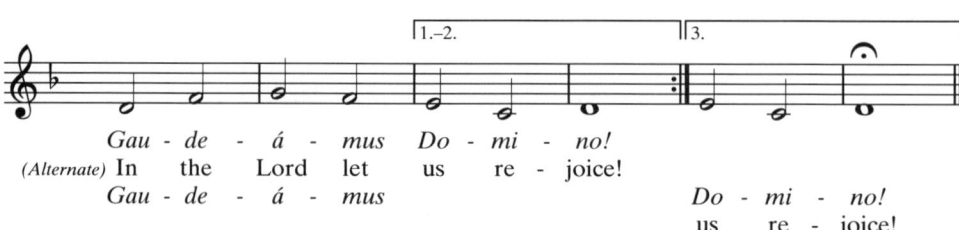

Gau - de - á - mus Do - mi - no!
(Alternate) In the Lord let us re - joice!
Gau - de - á - mus Do - mi - no!
us re - joice!

Text: Delores Dufner, O.S.B. © 1983 Sisters of St. Benedict, St. Joseph, MN 56374
Music: © 1983 Jay F. Hunstiger, 4545 Wichita Trail, Medina, MN 55340

Dedicated to the people of Holy Name Parish, Bimini, Bahamas

This Is God's Holy Temple 68

REFRAIN

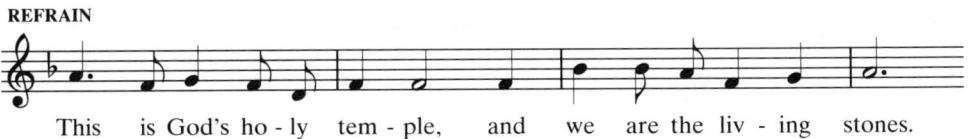
This is God's ho-ly tem-ple, and we are the liv-ing stones.

Let us bow down in prayer, sing-ing God's prais - es!

VERSE 1

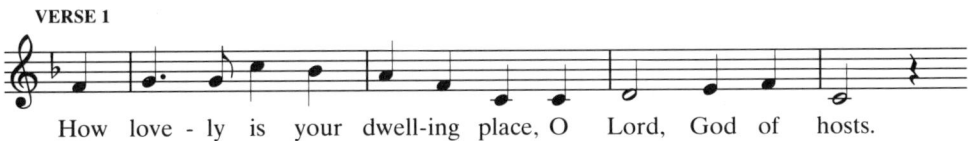
How love-ly is your dwell-ing place, O Lord, God of hosts.

rit.   *To Refrain*

My soul is long-ing and yearn-ing, is yearn-ing for the courts of the Lord.

VERSES 2 & 3

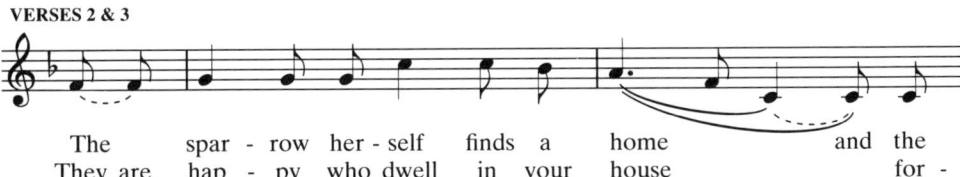
The spar-row her-self finds a home and the
They are hap-py who dwell in your house for -

swal-low a nest for her brood; she lays her young by your
ev - er sing-ing your praise. They are hap-py whose strength is in

rit.   *To Refrain*

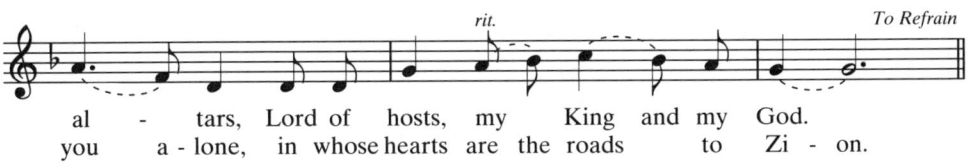
al - tars, Lord of hosts, my King and my God.
you a - lone, in whose hearts are the roads to Zi - on.

Text: Refrain: Tobias Colgan, O.S.B. © 1988 St. Meinrad Archabbey, St. Meinrad, IN 47577; vv. Psalm 84: 2–3ab; 4; 5–6, alt. © 1963–1986 Ladies of the Grail (England). Used by permission of GIA Publications, Inc., Chicago, IL, exclusive agent. All rights reserved.
Music: Tobias Colgan, O.S.B. © 1988 St. Meinrad Archabbey, St. Meinrad, IN 47577

69 This Is the Day the Lord Has Made

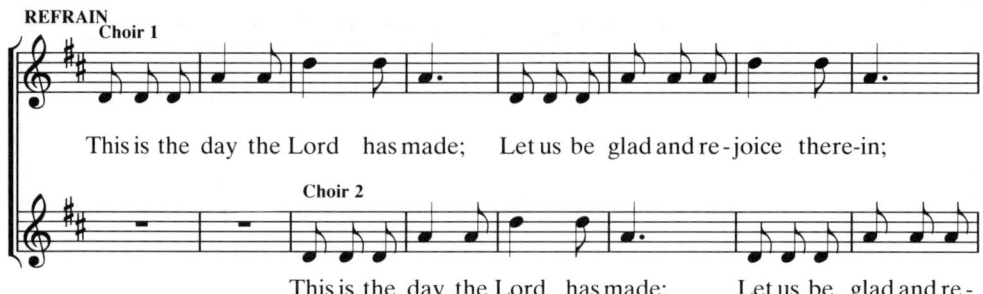

Text: Based on Gospel text for Easter Sequence © 1981 Jane Klimisch, O.S.B., Sacred Heart Convent, Yankton, SD 57078
Music: Jane Klimisch, O.S.B. © 1981 Sacred Heart Convent, Yankton, SD 57078

VERSE 2

VERSE 3

Alleluia
ALLELUIA
Alleluia
Alleluia alleluia
ALLELUIA
Alleluia ALLELUIA

70 This Is What the Lord Asks of You

REFRAIN

This is what the Lord asks of you: to act just-ly,

to love ten-der-ly and to walk hum-bly with your God.

VERSES

1. My song is of mer - cy and jus - tice;
2. I will walk with a blame-less heart
3. I look to the faith-ful in the land

    I sing to you, O Lord.
with - in my house, O Lord.
that they may dwell with me.

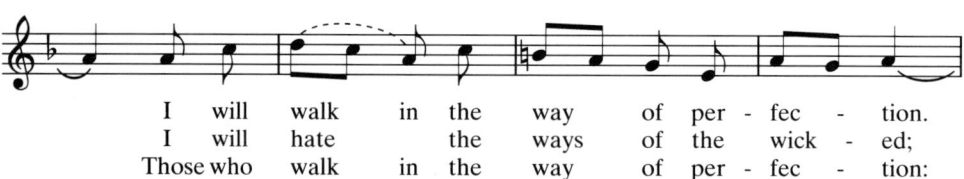

    I will walk in the way of per - fec - tion.
I will hate the ways of the wick - ed;
Those who walk in the way of per - fec - tion:

D.S.

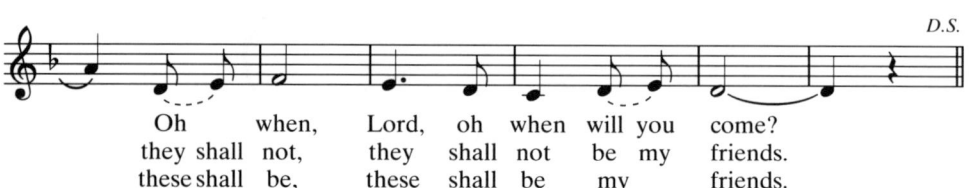

Oh when, Lord, oh when will you come?
they shall not, they shall not be my friends.
these shall be, these shall be my friends.

Text: Refrain: Tobias Colgan, O.S.B. © 1984 St. Meinrad Archabbey, St. Meinrad, IN 47577; vv. Psalm 101: 1–2; 3cd; 6, alt. © 1963–1986 Ladies of the Grail (England). Used by permission of GIA Publications, Inc., Chicago, IL, exclusive agent. All rights reserved.
Music: Tobias Colgan, O.S.B. © 1984 St. Meinrad Archabbey, St. Meinrad, IN 47577

Though the Hills Be Wrapped in Silence 71

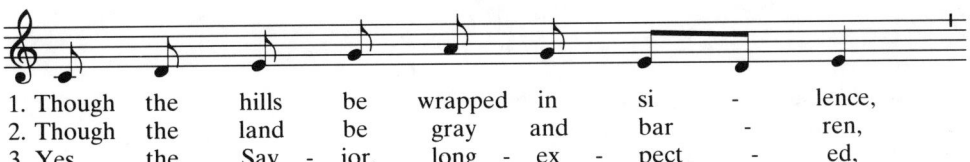

1. Though the hills be wrapped in si - lence,
2. Though the land be gray and bar - ren,
3. Yes, the Sav - ior, long - ex - pect - ed,

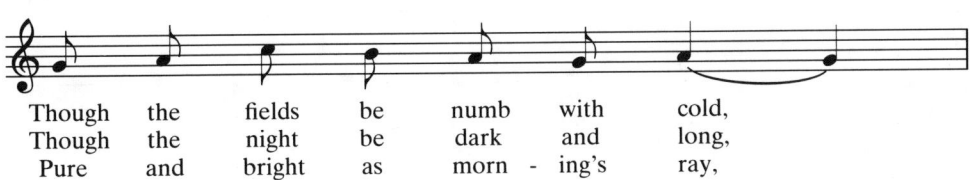

Though the fields be numb with cold,
Though the night be dark and long,
Pure and bright as morn - ing's ray,

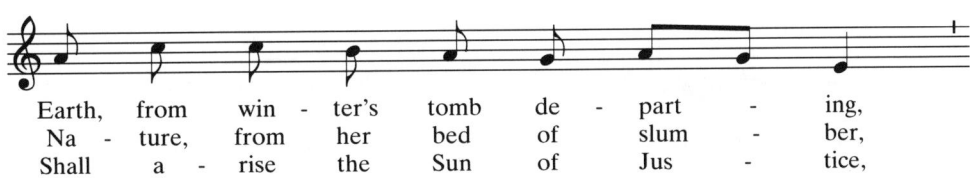

Earth, from win - ter's tomb de - part - ing,
Na - ture, from her bed of slum - ber,
Shall a - rise the Sun of Jus - tice,

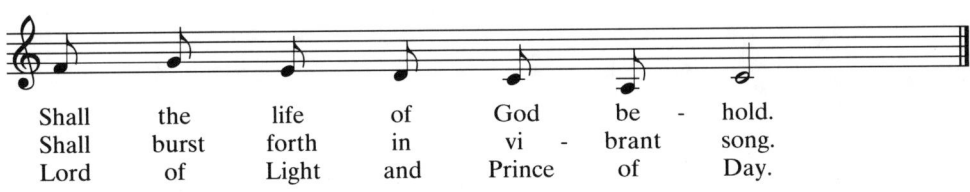

Shall the life of God be - hold.
Shall burst forth in vi - brant song.
Lord of Light and Prince of Day.

Text: Becket Gerald Senchur, O.S.B. © 1978 St. Vincent Archabbey, Latrobe, PA 15650
Music: Becket Gerald Senchur, O.S.B. © 1978 St. Vincent Archabbey, Latrobe, PA 15650

72 To the Wedding Feast God Calls Us

Text: Delores Dufner, O.S.B. © 1984 Sisters of St. Benedict, St. Joseph, MN 56374
Music: © 1984 Jay F. Hunstiger, 4545 Wichita Trail, Medina, MN 55540

BROKEN BREAD
87 87 D

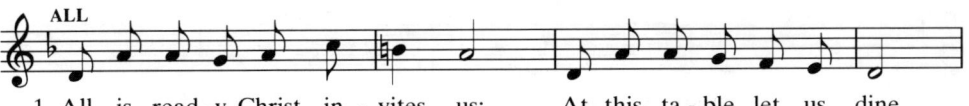
1. All is read-y, Christ in-vites us: At this ta-ble let us dine.

From the tree of life God feeds us Rich-est food and fin-est wine!

5. Risen Jesus, walk beside us,
   Show us all that you have said.
   Friend and Teacher, let us know you
   In the breaking of the bread.

6. You have made your home among us;
   All you promised, you will do.
   From the well of life we drink now;
   Come, make your creation new!

7. Face to face our God will meet us;
   We will not need lamps again.
   Star of Morning, Sun of Justice,
   Come, Lord Jesus, Amen!

73 Today Is Born Our Savior

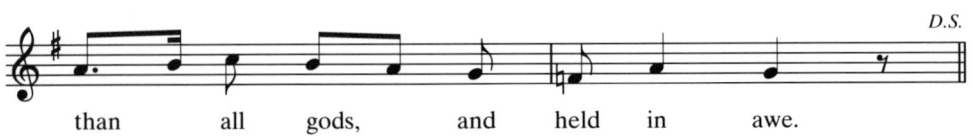

Text: English tr. of the refrain from the LECTIONARY FOR MASS © 1969, ICEL. Psalm 96: 1–4; 11–12 © 1986 A NEW METRICAL PSALTER by Christopher L. Webber. Used with permission.
Music: Kilian K. Sullivan, O.S.B. © 1988 Conception Abbey, Conception, MO 64433

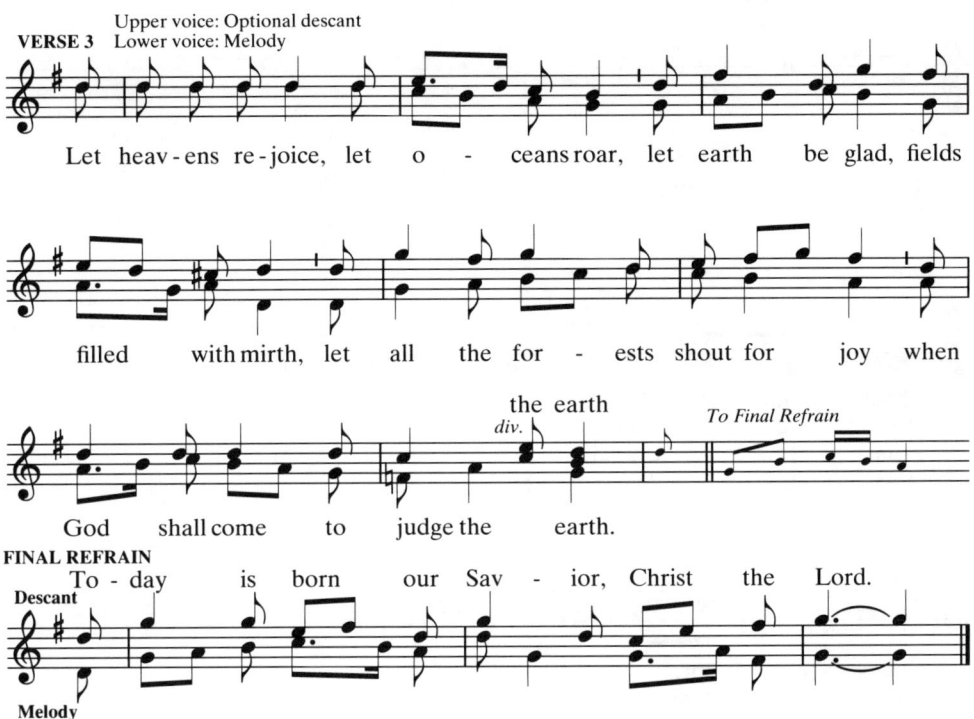

74 Unto Us a Child Is Given

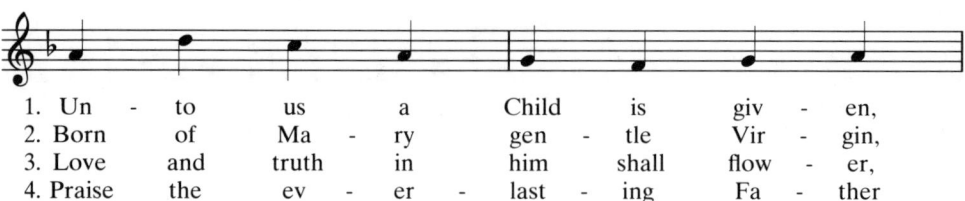

1. Un - to us a Child is giv - en,
2. Born of Ma - ry gen - tle Vir - gin,
3. Love and truth in him shall flow - er,
4. Praise the ev - er - last - ing Fa - ther

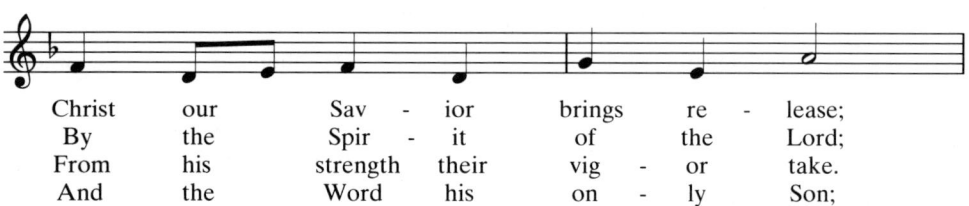

Christ our Sav - ior brings re - lease;
By the Spir - it of the Lord;
From his strength their vig - or take.
And the Word his on - ly Son;

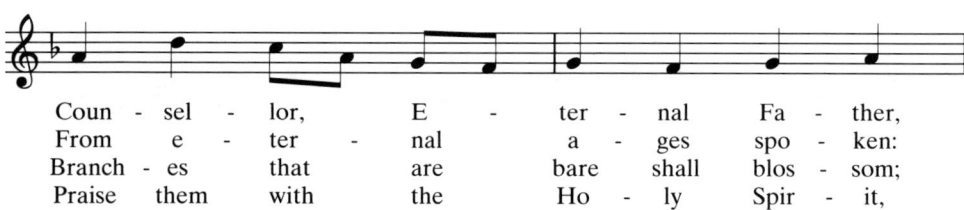

Coun - sel - lor, E - ter - nal Fa - ther,
From e - ter - nal a - ges spo - ken:
Branch - es that are bare shall blos - som;
Praise them with the Ho - ly Spir - it,

Word made flesh and Prince of Peace.
This the might - y Fa - ther's Word.
Joy that slept be - gins to wake.
Per - fect Trin - i - ty in One.

Text: © 1974 Stanbrook Abbey, Worcester, England, adapt.
Music: Aaron Jensen, O.S.B. © 1980 Assumption Abbey, Richardton, ND 58652

Wait When the Seed Is Planted 75

1. Wait when the seed is plant-ed, Wait for the rain to fall;
2. Hope when the sun is set-ting, Hope through the dark of night;
3. Trust in the new spring's prom-ise, Trust through the sum-mer's heat;

Wait for the rest-less green sprout, Wait while the plant grows tall.
Hope though the moon is wan-ing, Hope as we long for light.
Trust in the dy-ing au-tumn, Trust through the win-ter sleet.

Wait for the com-ing Sav-ior, Wait through the heart's slow race;
Hope for the com-ing Sav-ior, Hope through the heart's slow race;
Trust in the com-ing Sav-ior, Trust in the heart's slow race;

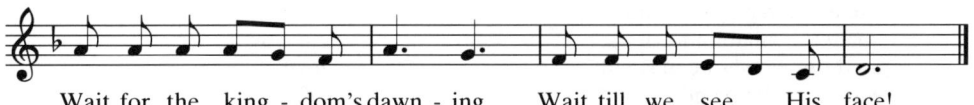

Wait for the king-dom's dawn-ing, Wait till we see His face!
Hope for the king-dom's dawn-ing, Hope till we see His face!
Trust in the king-dom's dawn-ing, Trust till we see His face!

Text: Delores Dufner, O.S.B. © 1983 Sisters of St. Benedict, St. Joseph, MN 56374
Music: © 1983 Jay F. Hunstiger, 4545 Wichita Trail, Medina, MN 55340

GAUDETE
76 76 D

76 Was It Not Needful

ANTIPHON

Was it not need-ful that Christ should suf-fer thus

and so en-ter in-to his glo - ry? Al - le - lu - ia.

VERSES

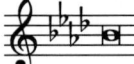

    1. Praise the Lord with the   lyre,
    2. For the word of the Lord is   upright,
    3. From where God sits enthroned the Lord looks   forth
    4. Behold, the eye of the Lord is on those who fear the Lord,
    5. Our soul waits for the   Lord;

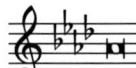

    make melody with the harp of ten   strings!
    and all God's work is done in   faithfulness.
    on all the inhabitants of the   earth;
    on those who hope in steadfast   love,
    who is our help and   shield.

    Sing to the Lord a new   song,
    The Lord loves righteousness and   justice,
    The Lord who fashions the hearts of them   all
    God delivers their souls from   death,
    Your steadfast love, O Lord, be up   -   on us,

    play skillfully on the strings, with loud   shouts.
    the earth is full of the steadfast love of the   Lord.
    and observes all their   deeds.
    and keeps them alive in   famine.
    even as we hope in   you.

Text: Antiphon: Isaac Borocz, O.S.B. © 1982 St. Anselm's Abbey, Washington, DC 20017; vv. Psalm 33: 2–5; 11–15; 18–22 from the Revised Standard Version of the Bible © 1946, 1952, 1971 by the Division of Christian Education of the National Council of Churches of Christ in the USA and used by permission. All rights reserved.
Music: Isaac Borocz, O.S.B. © 1982 St. Anselm's Abbey, Washington, DC 20017

We Come Before You, Lord 77

REFRAIN *Confidently*

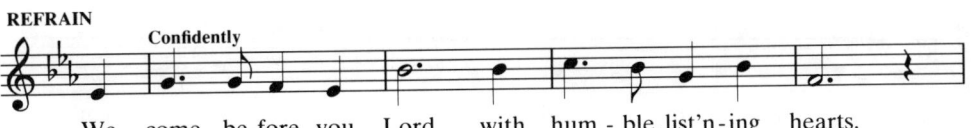

We come be-fore you, Lord, with hum-ble, list'n-ing hearts.

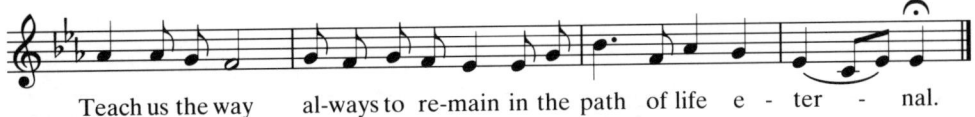

Teach us the way al-ways to re-main in the path of life e-ter-nal.

VERSES

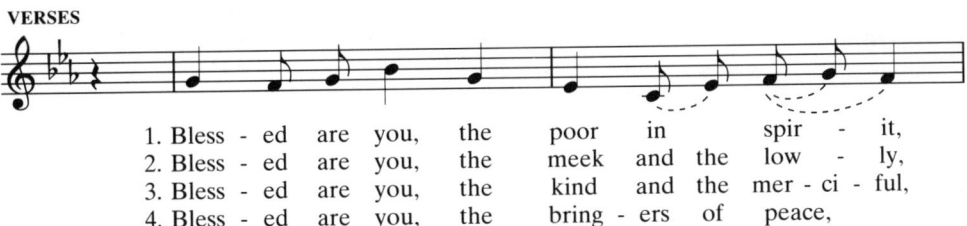

1. Bless-ed are you, the poor in spir-it,
2. Bless-ed are you, the meek and the low-ly,
3. Bless-ed are you, the kind and the mer-ci-ful,
4. Bless-ed are you, the bring-ers of peace,

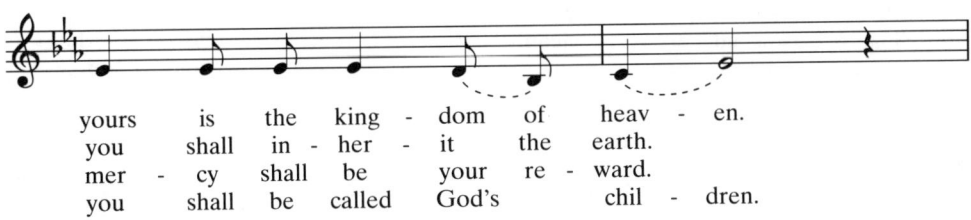

yours is the king-dom of heav-en.
you shall in-her-it the earth.
mer-cy shall be your re-ward.
you shall be called God's chil-dren.

Bless-ed are you who weep and mourn,
Bless-ed are you who thirst for jus-tice,
Bless-ed are you, the pure in heart,
Bless-ed are you who bear with trials,

To Refrain

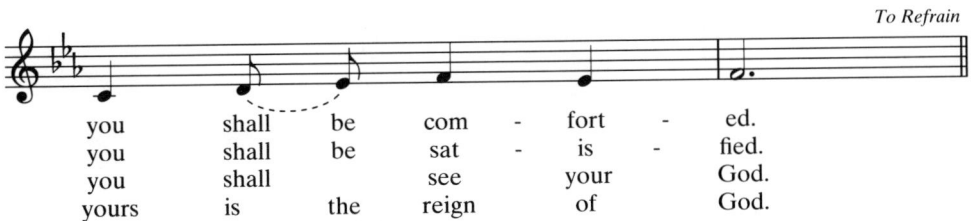

you shall be com-fort-ed.
you shall be sat-is-fied.
you shall see your God.
yours is the reign of God.

Text: Tobias Colgan, O.S.B. © 1986 St. Meinrad Archabbey, St. Meinrad, IN 47577
Music: Tobias Colgan, O.S.B. © 1986 St. Meinrad Archabbey, St. Meinrad, IN 47577

78 We Now Recall the Saving Death

1. We now recall the saving death
2. His death— what hope and peace it yields!
3. Yes, Christ, the humble Lamb of God,
4. So may the death of Christ, our Lord,

Of Christ, our Lord and Brother,
What freedom-filled salvation!
Sin's Victim marked for slaughter,
Inspire our thoughts and feelings,

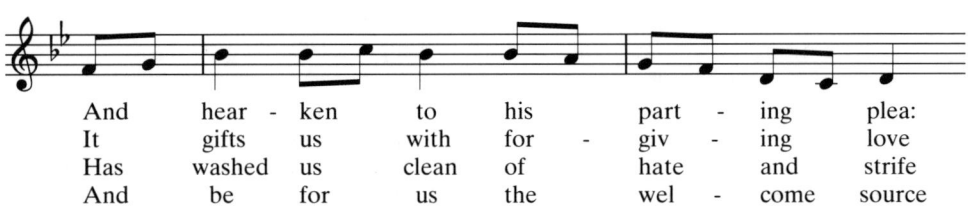

And hearken to his parting plea:
It gifts us with forgiving love
Has washed us clean of hate and strife
And be for us the welcome source

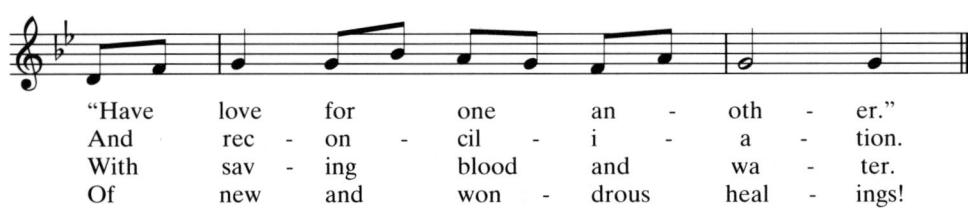

"Have love for one another."
And reconciliation.
With saving blood and water.
Of new and wondrous healings!

Text: Becket Gerald Senchur, O.S.B. © 1983 St. Vincent Archabbey, Latrobe, PA 15650
Music: Becket Gerald Senchur, O.S.B. © 1983 St. Vincent Archabbey, Latrobe, PA 15650

We Offer Prayer in Sorrow, Lord 79

1. We of-fer pray'r in sor-row, Lord, As-sist our frail be-
2. O com-fort us, we do be-lieve But find the way so
3. Re-ceive in-to your dwell-ing place All those whose lives have
4. We praise you, Fa-ther, Lord of Light, We praise you through our

liev - ing. Make strong in us those pow'r - ful words To
dark - ened. We miss the ones we do not see. The
end - ed. For - give their sins and give that peace For
sad - ness. We praise you, ris - en Je - sus Christ, Who

Mar - tha in her griev - ing: "Your bro - ther, though now
pain of life is sharp - ened. O come with com - fort,
which they were in - tend - ed. You died, O Lord, that
tri - umphed o - ver dark - ness. We praise you, Spir - it

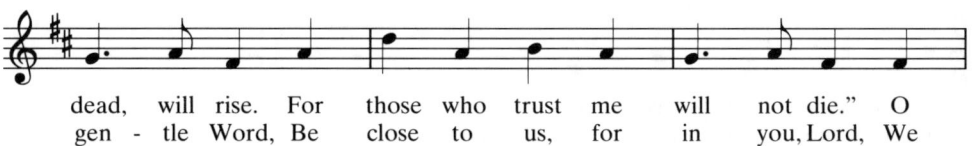

dead, will rise. For those who trust me will not die." O
gen - tle Word, Be close to us, for in you, Lord, We
they might live, Have mer - cy, in your love for - give, For -
of them both, O come with glad - ness, give us hope, And

hear these words of plead - ing.
find our own de - part - ed.
give where they of - fend - ed.
mi - ti - gate death's harsh - ness. A - men.

Text: Ralph Wright, O.S.B. © 1989 GIA Publications Inc., Chicago, IL. All rights reserved.
Music: Orgelchoralbuch zum evangelischen, 1966   ICH STEH' AN DEINER KRIPPE

80 We Praise You, Lord, with Joy This Day

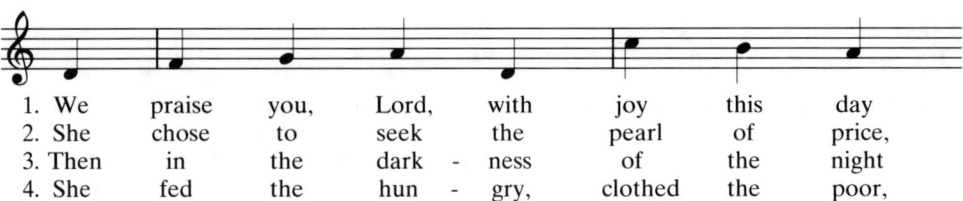

1. We praise you, Lord, with joy this day
2. She chose to seek the pearl of price,
3. Then in the dark - ness of the night
4. She fed the hun - gry, clothed the poor,

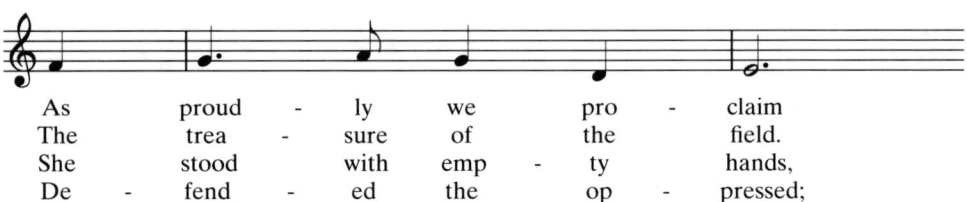

As proud - ly we pro - claim
The trea - sure of the field.
She stood with emp - ty hands,
De - fend - ed the op - pressed;

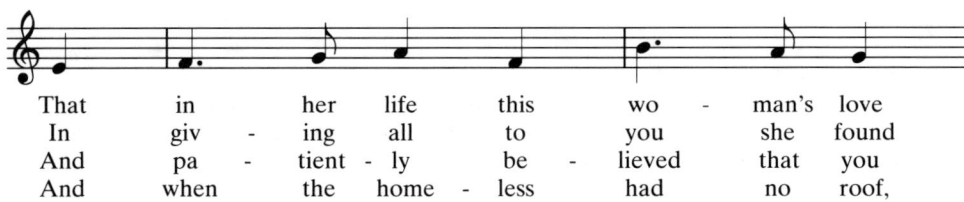

That in her life this wo - man's love
In giv - ing all to you she found
And pa - tient - ly be - lieved that you
And when the home - less had no roof,

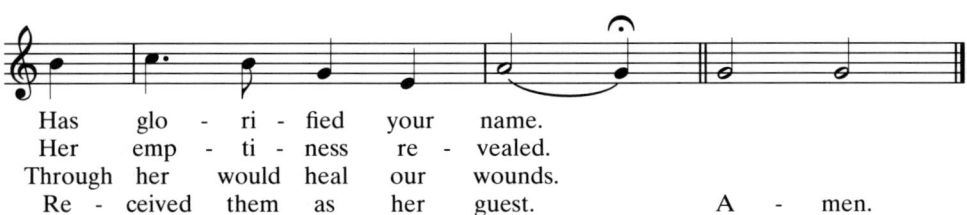

Has glo - ri - fied your name.
Her emp - ti - ness re - vealed.
Through her would heal our wounds.
Re - ceived them as her guest. A - men.

5. Beyond the darkest hour of doubt
   She made your Word her home;
   The storms of arrogance and strife
   Were stilled before her calm.

6. So on this day we praise you, Lord,
   Good Father, servant Son,
   O in your Spirit may this praise
   Keep us forever one.

Text: Ralph Wright, O.S.B. v. 1 © 1989 GIA Publications, Inc. Chicago, IL. All rights reserved. Vv. 2–6: © St. Louis Abbey, St. Louis, MO 63141
Music: Tobias Colgan, O.S.B. © 1984 St. Meinrad Archabbey, St. Meinrad, IN 47577

We Stand to Greet the Dawning Day 81

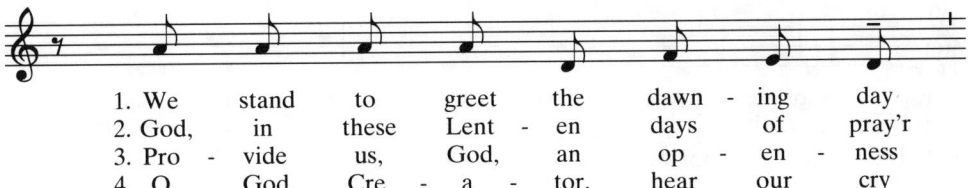

1. We stand to greet the dawn - ing day
2. God, in these Lent - en days of pray'r
3. Pro - vide us, God, an op - en - ness
4. O God, Cre - a - tor, hear our cry

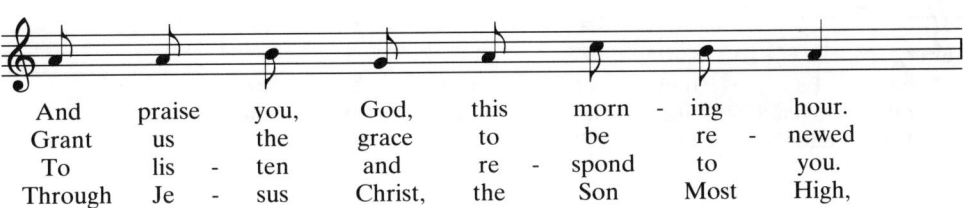

And praise you, God, this morn - ing hour.
Grant us the grace to be re - newed
To lis - ten and re - spond to you.
Through Je - sus Christ, the Son Most High,

Turn dark - ness in - to light be - fore us
In our bap - tis - mal con - se - cra - tion:
May this our Lent - en fast be filled
Whom with the Spir - it we a - dore

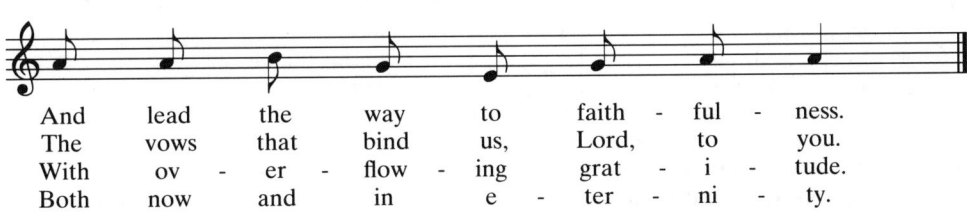

And lead the way to faith - ful - ness.
The vows that bind us, Lord, to you.
With ov - er - flow - ing grat - i - tude.
Both now and in e - ter - ni - ty.

Text: Monika Ellis, O.S.B. © 1989 St. Placid Priory, Lacey, WA 98506
Music: Plainchant, Mode 1; acc. Cecile Gertken, O.S.B. © 1989 Sisters of St. Benedict, St. Joseph, MN 56374

JESU DULCIS MEMORIA

82 We Thank You, Father, Lord of All

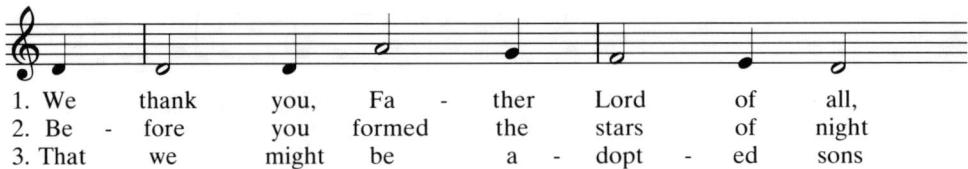

1. We thank you, Fa - ther Lord of all,
2. Be - fore you formed the stars of night
3. That we might be a - dopt - ed sons

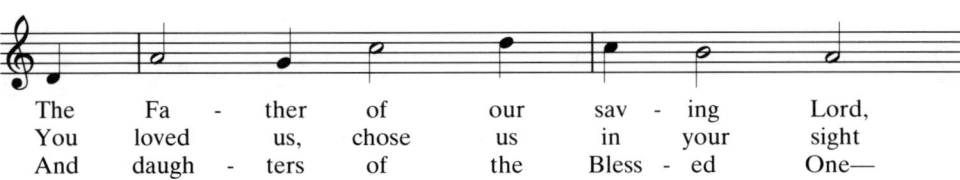

The Fa - ther of our sav - ing Lord,
You loved us, chose us in your sight
And daugh - ters of the Bless - ed One—

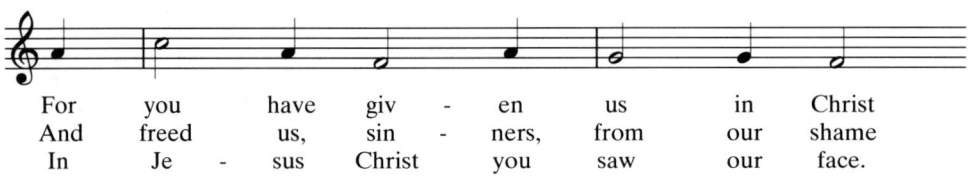

For you have giv - en us in Christ
And freed us, sin - ners, from our shame
In Je - sus Christ you saw our face.

The bless - ing of e - ter - nal life.
To love and glo - ri - fy your name.
O praise such glo - ry, praise such grace! A - men.

4. For in his death we have been saved
From death and sin and Satan's claims,
Redeemed by your abundant love
And purified in Jesus' blood.

5. To know and joyfully declare
Your wise design beyond compare,
That all in Christ, the risen Lord,
Should one day be at last restored.

Text: Ralph Wright, O.S.B. © 1984 St. Louis Abbey, St. Louis, MO 63141

WIR DANKEN GOTT
88 88

What Feast of Love 83

1. What feast of love is of-fered here, What ban-quet come from heav - en?
2. What light of truth is of-fered here, What cov - e - nant from heav - en?
3. What wine of love is of-fered here, What crim-son drink from heav - en?

What food of ev - er - last - ing life, What gra - cious gift is giv - en?
What hope of ev - er - last - ing life, What won - drous word is giv - en?
What stream of ev - er - last - ing life, What pre - cious blood is giv - en?

This, this is Christ the King, The bread come down from heav - en.
This, this is Christ the King, The Sun come down from heav - en.
This, this is Christ the King, The sweet-est wine of heav - en.

O taste and see and sing! How sweet the man - na giv - en!
O see, and, list - 'ning, sing! The Word of God is giv - en!
O taste and see and sing! The Son of God is giv - en!

Text: Delores Dufner, O.S.B. © 1986 Sisters of St. Benedict, St. Joseph, MN 56374
Music: English melody, 16th C.

GREENSLEEVES
87 87 68 67

84 When All the Stars of Morning Sang

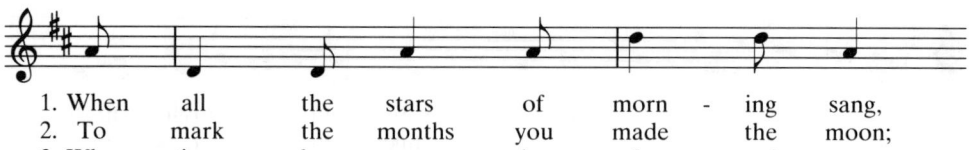

1. When all the stars of morning sang,
2. To mark the months you made the moon;
3. When time has run its final course,

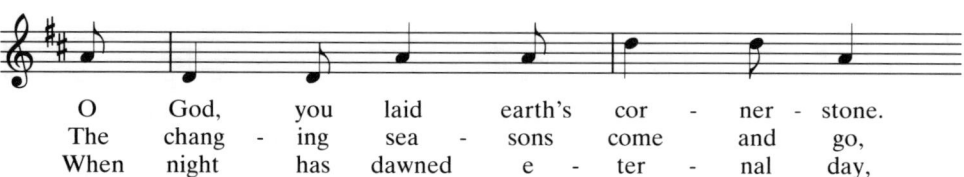

O God, you laid earth's corner-stone.
The changing seasons come and go,
When night has dawned eternal day,

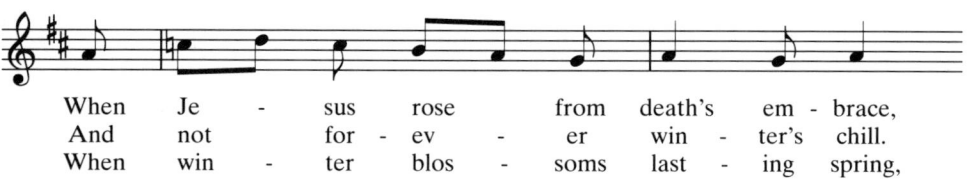

When Jesus rose from death's embrace,
And not forever winter's chill.
When winter blossoms lasting spring,

The sun in radiant glory shone.
See, seeds asleep beneath the snow!
Then shall we need no longer pray:

O re-create what sin has marred;
O re-create what sin has marred;
O re-create what sin has marred;

Restore our spirits like the dawn.
Restore our spirits like the spring.
Restore our spirits by your breath.

Text: Delores Dufner, O.S.B. © 1984 Sisters of St. Benedict, St. Joseph, MN 56374
Music: © 1984 Jay F. Hunstiger, 4545 Wichita Trail, Medina, MN 55340

FULGERE
L M D

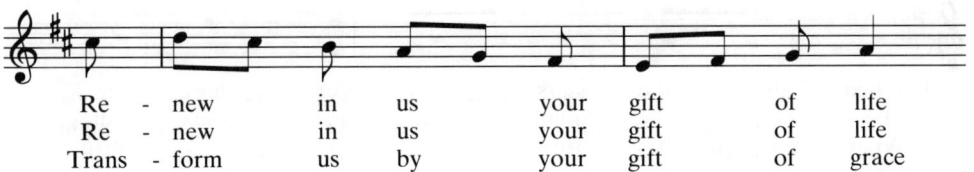

Re - new in us your gift of life
Re - new in us your gift of life
Trans - form us by your gift of grace

And thrill our hearts to joy - ful song.
And teach our hearts once more to sing.
And bring new life from pain and death.

85 When Evening Falls and Labors Cease

1. When evening falls and labors cease,
2. As dawn will surely follow night,
3. Like birds returning to their nest,
4. Safe sheltered by your mighty wings,

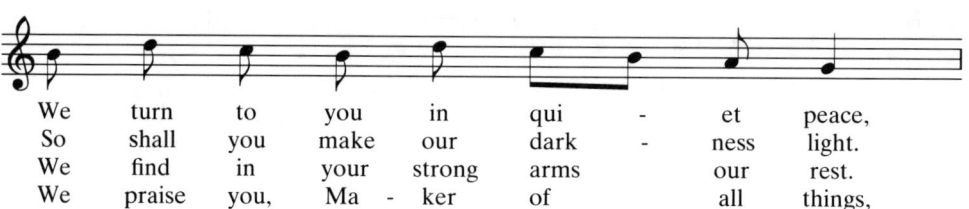

We turn to you in quiet peace,
So shall you make our darkness light.
We find in your strong arms our rest.
We praise you, Maker of all things,

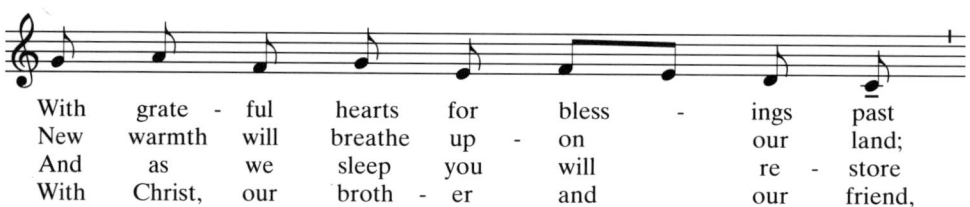

With grateful hearts for blessings past
New warmth will breathe upon our land;
And as we sleep you will restore
With Christ, our brother and our friend,

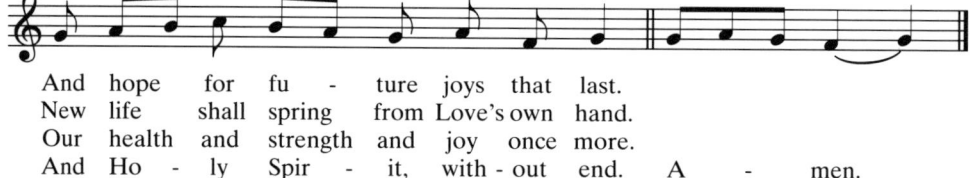

And hope for future joys that last.
New life shall spring from Love's own hand.
Our health and strength and joy once more.
And Holy Spirit, without end. A - men.

Text: Delores Dufner, O.S.B., © 1986 Sisters of St. Benedict, St. Joseph, MN 56374
Music: Plainchant, Mode 8, LIBER HYMNARIUS; acc. Cecile Gertken, O.S.B.
© 1989 Sisters of St. Benedict, St. Joseph, MN 56374

JESU CORONA VIRGINUM
88 88

When from Bondage We Are Summoned 86

VERSES

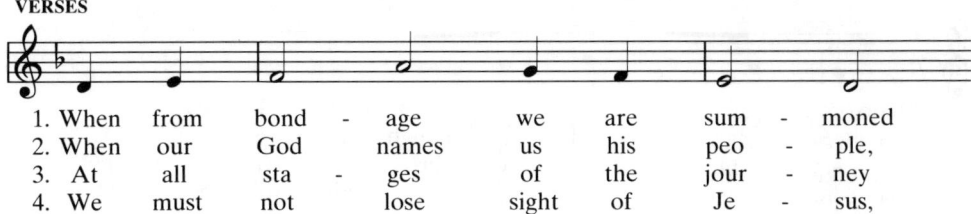

1. When from bond - age we are sum - moned
2. When our God names us his peo - ple,
3. At all sta - ges of the jour - ney
4. We must not lose sight of Je - sus,

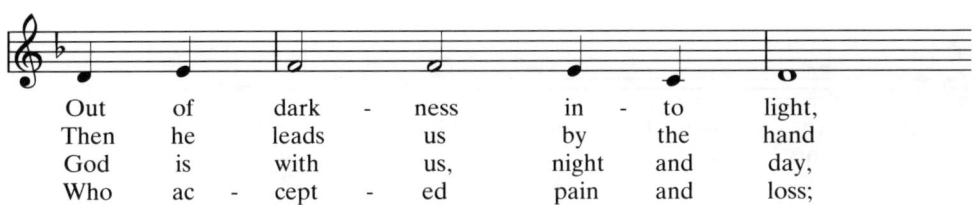

Out of dark - ness in - to light,
Then he leads us by the hand
God is with us, night and day,
Who ac - cept - ed pain and loss;

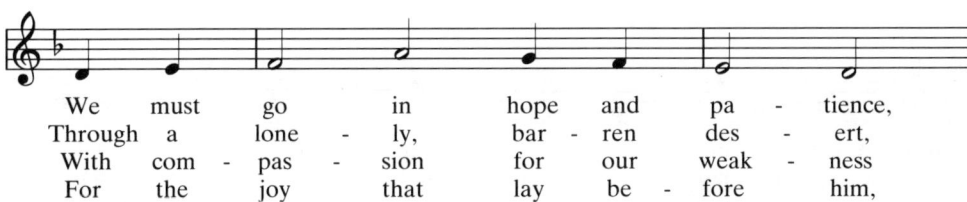

We must go in hope and pa - tience,
Through a lone - ly, bar - ren des - ert,
With com - pas - sion for our weak - ness
For the joy that lay be - fore him,

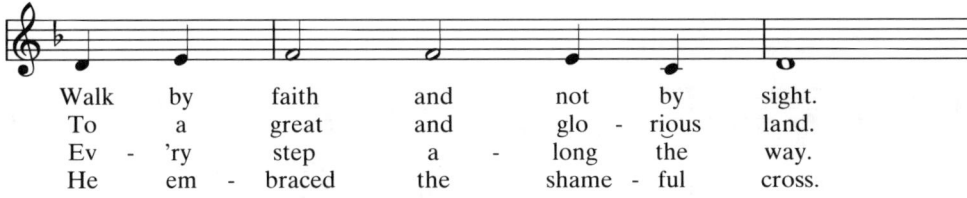

Walk by faith and not by sight.
To a great and glo - rious land.
Ev - 'ry step a - long the way.
He em - braced the shame - ful cross.

REFRAIN

Let us throw off all that hin - ders; Let us run the race to win!

Let us has - ten to our home-land And, re - joic - ing, en - ter in.

5. See the prize to which God calls us:
   Life on high in Christ the Lord.
   Let us fix our eyes on Jesus
   And in faith cling to his word.

Text: Delores Dufner, O.S.B. © 1984 Sisters of St. Benedict, St. Joseph, MN 56374
Music: © 1984 Jay F. Hunstiger, 4545 Wichita Trail, Medina, MN 55340

ST. GEORGE
87 87 D

87 When Peace Like a River

1. When peace like a river attends all my way,
2. Though Satan should buffet, though trials should come,
3. My sin— O the bliss of this glorious thought—
4. And, Lord, haste the day when our faith will be sight,

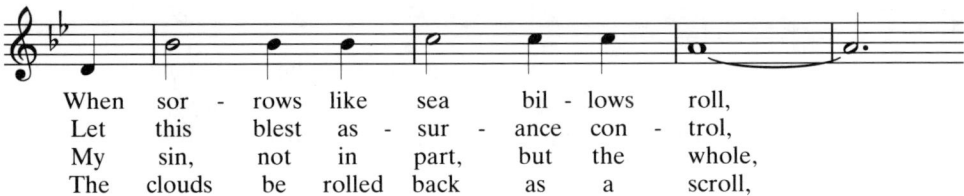

When sorrows like sea billows roll,
Let this blest assurance control,
My sin, not in part, but the whole,
The clouds be rolled back as a scroll,

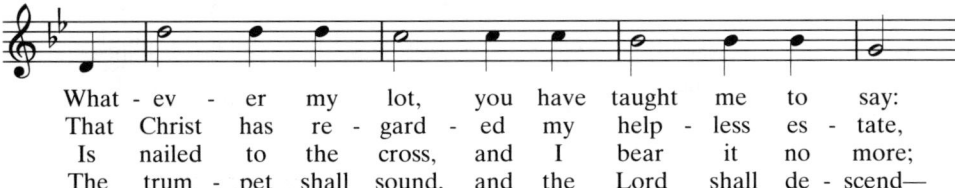

Whatever my lot, you have taught me to say:
That Christ has regarded my helpless estate,
Is nailed to the cross, and I bear it no more;
The trumpet shall sound, and the Lord shall descend—

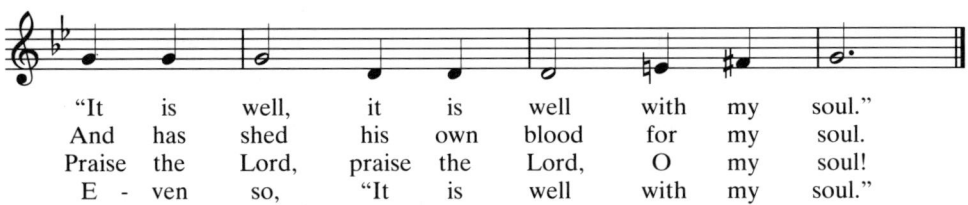

"It is well, it is well with my soul."
And has shed his own blood for my soul.
Praise the Lord, praise the Lord, O my soul!
Even so, "It is well with my soul."

Text: Horatio G. Spafford, 1828–1888, alt.
Music: Becket Gerald Senchur, O.S.B. © 1980 St. Vincent Archabbey, Latrobe, PA 15650

Who Are These, Like Stars Appearing 88

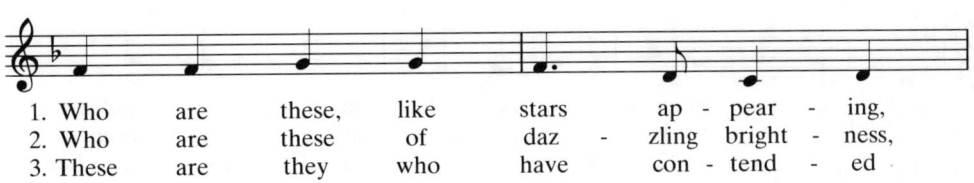

1. Who are these, like stars ap - pear - ing,
2. Who are these of daz - zling bright - ness,
3. These are they who have con - tend - ed

These be - fore God's throne who stand?
These in God's own truth ar - rayed,
For their Sav - ior's hon - or long,

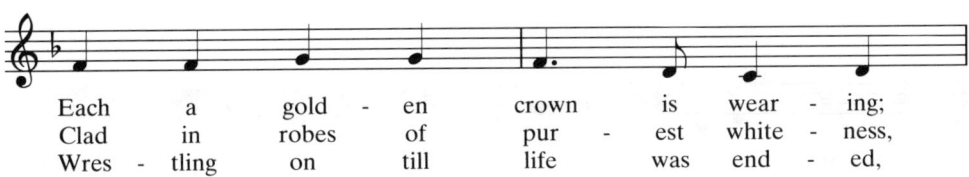

Each a gold - en crown is wear - ing;
Clad in robes of pur - est white - ness,
Wres - tling on till life was end - ed,

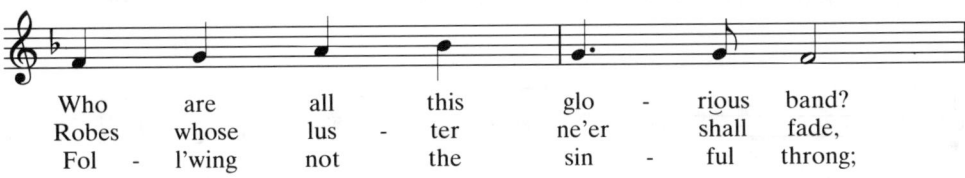

Who are all this glo - rious band?
Robes whose lus - ter ne'er shall fade,
Fol - l'wing not the sin - ful throng;

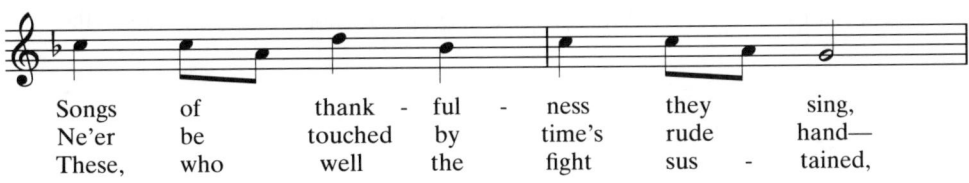

Songs of thank - ful - ness they sing,
Ne'er be touched by time's rude hand—
These, who well the fight sus - tained,

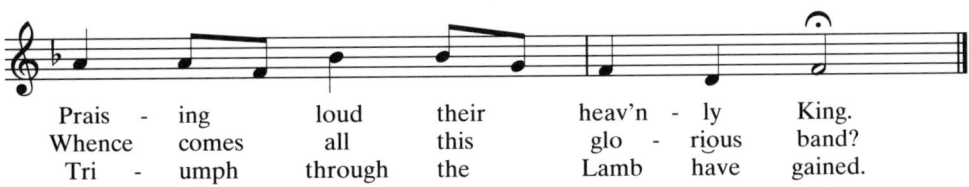

Prais - ing loud their heav'n - ly King.
Whence comes all this glo - rious band?
Tri - umph through the Lamb have gained.

Text: Theobald Heinrich Schenk, 1656–1727; tr. Frances Elizabeth Cox, 1812–1897, alt.
Music: Tobias Colgan, O.S.B. © 1985 St. Meinrad Archabbey, St. Meinrad, IN 47577

QUIENES SON
87 87 77

89 You Are God, We Chant Your Praises

1. You are God, we chant your prais-es; We ac-claim you Lord and King.
2. Blest a-pos-tles, ho-ly pro-phets, White-robed mar-tyrs praise your name,
3. You, O Christ are King of glo-ry. You, the Fa-ther's on-ly Son,
4. Come then, Lord, sus-tain your peo-ple, Ran-somed by your blood from strife.

To the Fa-ther ev-er-last-ing, An-gels and all crea-tures sing:
And the Church with ju-bi-la-tion Here on earth your might ac-claim.
Born for us of low-ly Vir-gin, O-ver death have tri-umph won.
Rank us with your saints in glo-ry To en-joy e-ter-nal life.

Ho-ly, ho-ly, ho-ly, ho-ly, God of po-wer, God of might!
Fa-ther o-ver all ma-jes-tic, Je-sus Christ your Son, our Lord
You have o-pened heav-en's king-dom To all those who in you trust.
Save us, Lord, your cho-sen peo-ple, Yours from all e-ter-ni-ty.

Earth and heav-en, all cre-a-tion Ra-di-ates your glo-ry bright.
And our Guide, the Ho-ly Spi-rit, E-qual-ly to be a-dored!
Seat-ed at God's right in glo-ry, You will judge us, Lord, most just.
Do not dis-ap-point us ev-er; All our hope is placed in thee.

May be used with HYFRODOL
IN BABILONE
HYMN TO JOY

Text: Matthew Leavy, O.S.B. © 1986 St. Anselm Abbey, Manchester, NH 03102

AUSTRIA
87 87 D

You Are the Way 90

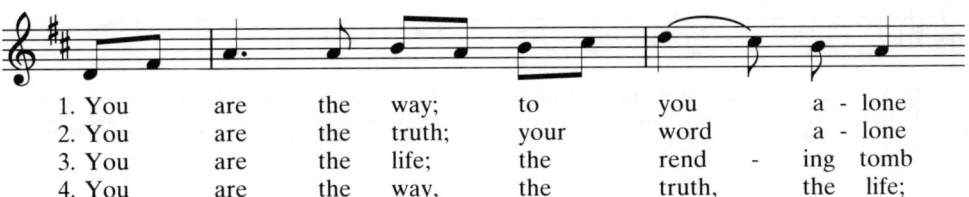

1. You are the way; to you a-lone
2. You are the truth; your word a-lone
3. You are the life; the rend-ing tomb
4. You are the way, the truth, the life;

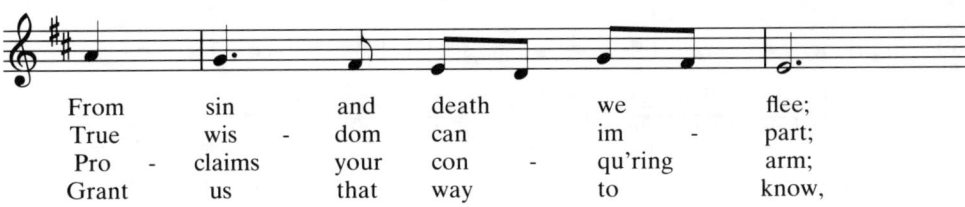

From sin and death we flee;
True wis-dom can im-part;
Pro-claims your con-qu'ring arm;
Grant us that way to know,

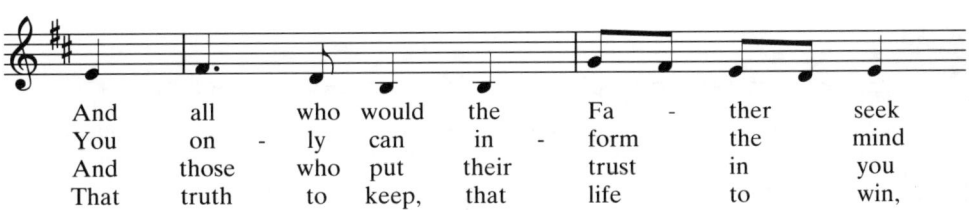

And all who would the Fa-ther seek
You on-ly can in-form the mind
And those who put their trust in you
That truth to keep, that life to win,

Must seek you faith-ful-ly.
And pu-ri-fy the heart.
Will nev-er come to harm.
Whose joys e-ter-nal flow.

Text: George Washington Doane, 1799–1859, alt.
Music: Tobias Colgan, O.S.B. © 1989 St. Meinrad Archabbey, St. Meinrad, IN 47577

91 Litany for Lent/Reconciliation

Text: Aurelius Boberek, O.S.B. © 1977 St. Meinrad Archabbey, St. Meinrad, IN 47577
Music: Traditional chant

That you would renew us in this sea-son.

℟. Lord, we ask you, hear our prayer.

Strengthen our acts of self-denial
    and prepare us for the PASchal Mystery.
That this offering of our worship
    may come from PRAYERful hearts.
Look with mercy on our weakness
    and forgive OUR offenses.
Grant peace throughout the world
    and unity to all CHRIStian people.
Visit this house in peace
    and teach us to live in LOVE and concord.
Increase the gifts of prayer among us
    that through purity of heart we may live IN your presence.
Confirm in our hearts the grace of OUR vocation.
Inspire us to seek you in siLENCE and solitude.
Console the suffering, comfort the dying,
    and take pity on all who ARE in need.
May our prayers and works reach out to the poor
    and to the innocent victims OF injustice.
Have mercy, and enlighten those who have
    not HEARD the Gospel.
May we work with all those of good will
    to achieve harmony and understanding with all our brothERS and sisters.

(For use during Lent)
That in the joy of the Holy Spirit
    we may live our lives in expectation of HOly Easter.

Christ, hear us! ℟. Christ, hear us!

To conclude, the *Lord, have mercy (Kyrie)* is intoned and repeated as at the beginning.

92 Litany of Mary of Nazareth

Text: PAX CHRISTI USA © 1987. Used with permission.
Music: S. Timothy Kirby, O.S.B. © 1987 St. Scholastica Priory, Duluth, MN 55811

93 Litany of Saints

We call up-on the Saints of God to join us in our prayer of praise.
to pray for us in time of need.
to join us in our prayer of thanks.

Anne, the moth-er of Ma - ry ℟. Join us in our prayer of praise.
Ma - ry, moth - er of us all, ℟. Pray for us in time of need.
℟. Join us in our prayer of thanks.

St. Ag - nes, ℟. Join us in our prayer of praise.
St. Ce - ci - lia,

Joan, the maid of Or - le - ans, ℟. Join us in our prayer of praise.
Tek - ak - with - a, In - dian maid,

St. Therese, little Flow - er, ℟. Join us in our prayer of praise.
St. Frances Ca - bri - ni,

Jo - seph, spouse of Ma - ry, ℟. Join us in our prayer of praise.
John, be - loved of Je - sus,

St. Paul, ℟. Join us in our prayer of praise.
St. Mat - thew,
St. Dom - i - nic,

Ho - ly Fath - er Ben - e - dict, ℟. Join us in our prayer of praise.
Fran - cis of As - si - si,
Vir - gin, mys - tic, Hil - de - garde,

Names of saints may be added or deleted.

Text: S. Timothy Kirby, O.S.B. © 1986 St. Scholastica Priory, Duluth, MN 55811
Music: S. Timothy Kirby, O.S.B. © 1986 St. Scholastica Priory, Duluth, MN 55811

St. Ber - nard, ℟. Join us in our prayer of praise.
St. Scho - las - ti - ca,
St. Gert - rude,

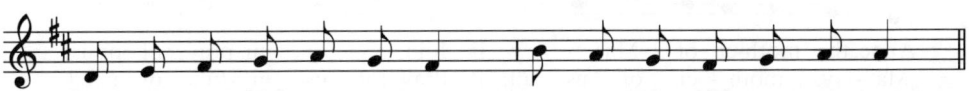
All you Ben - e - dic - tine Saints, ℟. Join us in our prayer of praise.

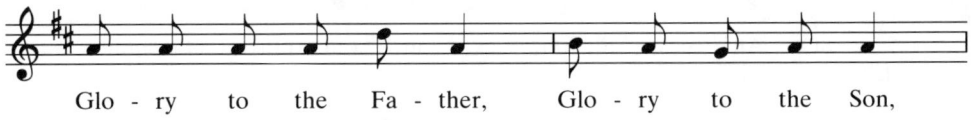
Glo - ry to the Fa - ther, Glo - ry to the Son,

Glo - ry to the Spir - it now and ev - er - more.

94 MASS IN E MINOR

94a Lord Have Mercy

Lord have mer - cy. Lord have mer - cy.

Christ have mer - cy. Christ have mer - cy.

Lord have mer - cy. Lord have mer - cy.

94b Glory to God

Glo - ry to God in the high - est and peace to his peo - ple on

earth. Lord God, heav-en-ly King, al - might - y God and Fa - ther, we

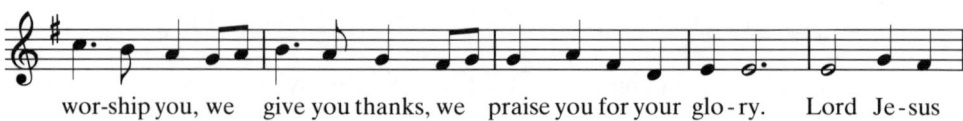
wor-ship you, we give you thanks, we praise you for your glo - ry. Lord Je - sus

Music: Mark Strassburger, O.S.B. © 1987 St. Bede Abbey, Peru, IL 61354

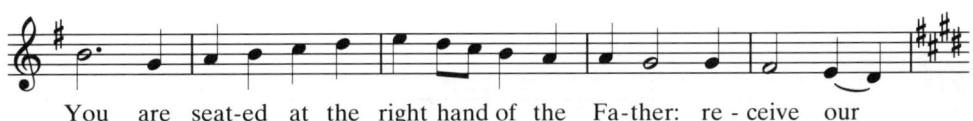

94c Holy

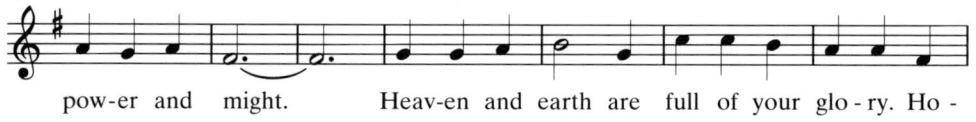

94d Memorial Acclamation

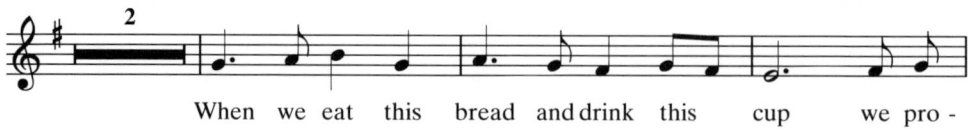

Amen 94e

Kingdom Acclamation 94f

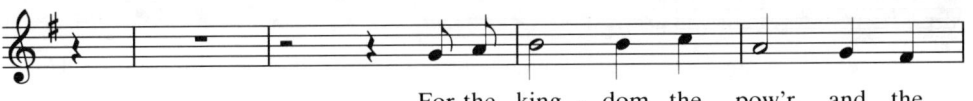

Lamb of God 94g

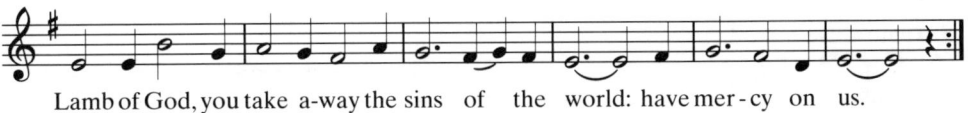

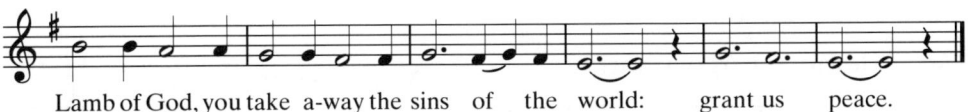

95 MASS OF HOPE

95a Lord Have Mercy

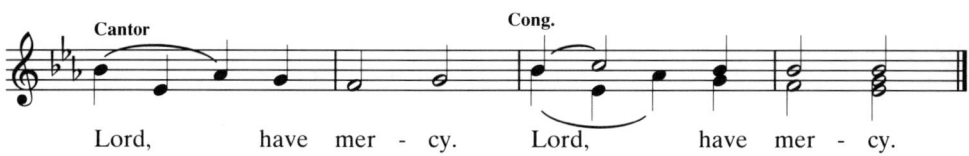

95b Glory to God

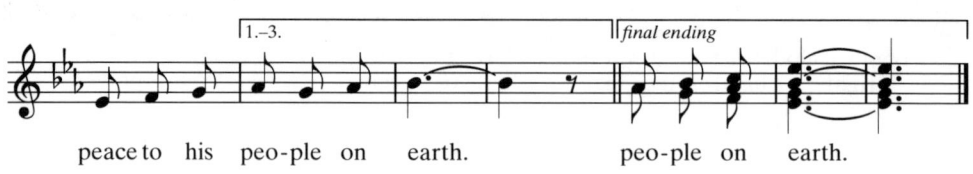

Music: Becket Gerald Senchur, O.S.B. © 1981 St. Vincent Archabbey, Latrobe, PA 15650

VERSE 2

VERSE 3

Holy 95c

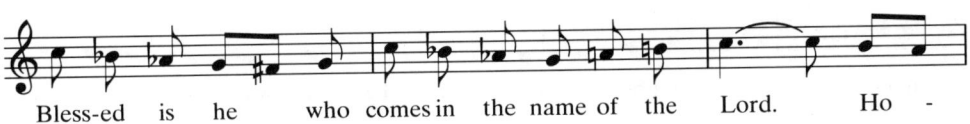

Memorial Acclamation 95d

95e Amen

95f Lamb of God

96 MASS ORDINARY XV

Lord Have Mercy 96a

Lord, have mer-cy. Christ, have mer-cy

Lord, have mer-cy. Lord, have mer-cy.

Glory to God 96b

Glo-ry to God in the high-est, and peace to his peo-ple on earth.

Lord God, heav-en-ly King, al-might-y God and Fa-ther.

We wor-ship you, we give you thanks, we praise you for your glo-ry.

Lord Je-sus Christ, on-ly Son of the Fa-ther. Lord God, Lamb of God,

you take a-way the sin of the world, have mer-cy on us.

Music: Plainchant, *DOMINATOR DEUS*, adapt. Cecile Gertken, O.S.B. and Bartholomew Sayles, O.S.B. © 1989 Sisters of St. Benedict, St. Joseph, MN 56374

Memorial Acclamation 96d

Amen 96e

Lamb of God 96f

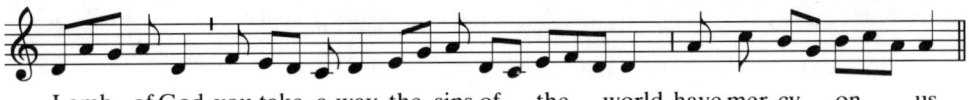

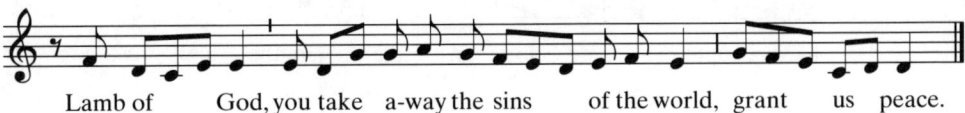

97 MASS IN E

97a Lord Have Mercy

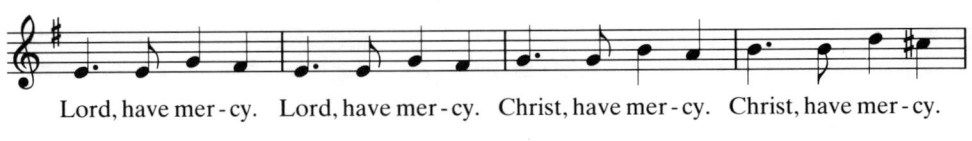
Lord, have mer-cy. Lord, have mer-cy. Christ, have mer-cy. Christ, have mer-cy.

Lord, have mer-cy. Lord, have mer - cy.

97b Holy

Ho - ly, ho - ly,

ho - ly Lord, God of pow - er and

might. Heav-en and earth are full of your glo - ry.

Ho - san - na in the high - est.

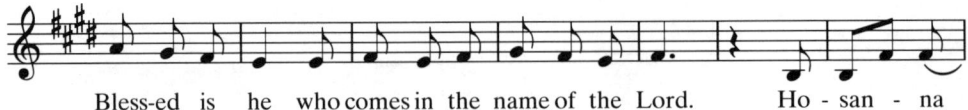
Bless-ed is he who comes in the name of the Lord. Ho - san - na

in the high - est, ho - san - na in the high - est.

Music: Edith Scholl, O.C.S.O. © 1989 Mount St. Mary's Abbey, Wrentham, MA 02093

Memorial Acclamation 97c

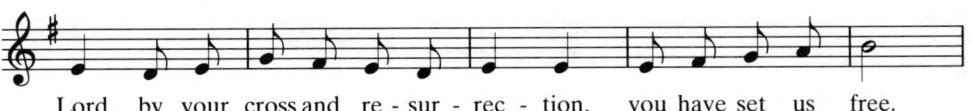

Amen 97d

Lamb of God 97e

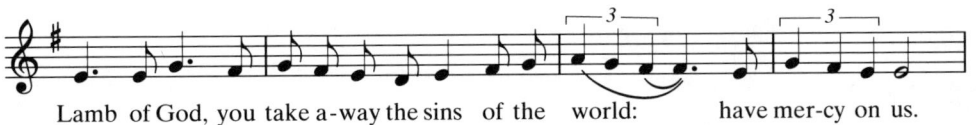

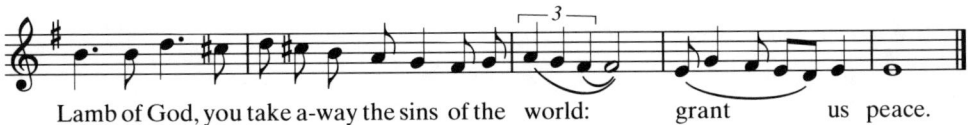

98 WEEKDAY MASS

98a Gospel Acclamation

Al - le - lu - ia, Al - le - lu - ia, Al - le - lu - ia!

98b Gospel Acclamation (Lent)

Praise to you, Lord Je - sus Christ, King of end - less glo - ry!

98c Holy

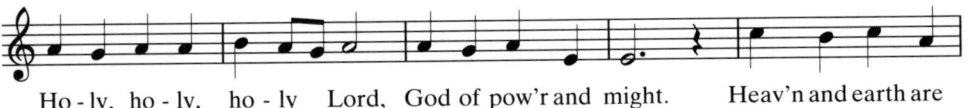

Ho - ly, ho - ly, ho - ly Lord, God of pow'r and might. Heav'n and earth are

full, are full of your glo - ry. Ho - san - na in the high - est.

Bless - ed is he who comes, who comes in the name of the Lord. Ho -

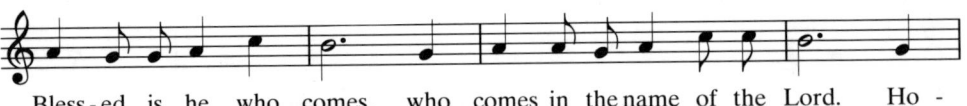

san - na in the high - est, in the high - est!

Music: Jane Klimisch, O.S.B. © 1989 Sacred Heart Convent, Yankton, SD 57078

Memorial Acclamation 98d

Amen 98e

Lamb of God 98f

99 MASS IN F

99a Holy

Ho-ly, ho-ly, ho-ly Lord, God of pow-er and

might. Heav'n and earth are full of your

glo-ry. Ho-san-na, Ho-san-na in the high-est.

Bless-ed is he who comes in the name of the Lord. Ho-

san-na, Ho-san-na in the high-est.

99b Memorial Acclamation

Christ has died, Christ is ris-en, Christ will come a-gain.

Christ has died, Christ is ris-en, Christ will come a-gain.

Music: Sean Duggan, O.S.B. © 1987 St. Joseph Abbey, St. Benedict, LA 70457

100 MISSA SIMPLEX

100a Holy

Ho - ly, ho - ly, ho - ly Lord, God of pow-er and might.

Heav-en and earth are full of your glo-ry. Ho-san - na in the high-est.

Bless-èd is he who comes in the name of the Lord. Ho-san - na in the high-est.

100b Memorial Acclamation

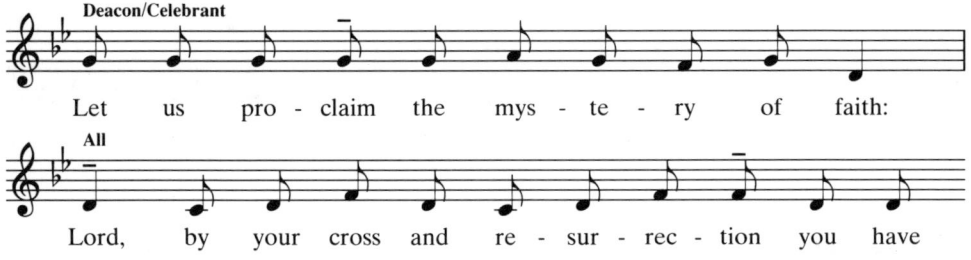

Deacon/Celebrant
Let us pro - claim the mys - te - ry of faith:

All
Lord, by your cross and re - sur - rec - tion you have set us free— you are the Sav - ior of the world!

100c Amen

Presider
For - ev - er and ev - er.

All
A - men, a - men!

Music: Basil Foote, O.S.B. © 1970 Westminster Abbey, Mission, British Columbia V2V 4J2

Lamb of God 100d

Lamb of God, you take a-way the sins of the world, have mer - cy on us.

Lamb of God, you take a-way the sins of the world, have mer - cy on us.

Lamb of God, you take a-way the sins of the world, grant us peace.

101 MASS OF ST. BENEDICT

101a Holy

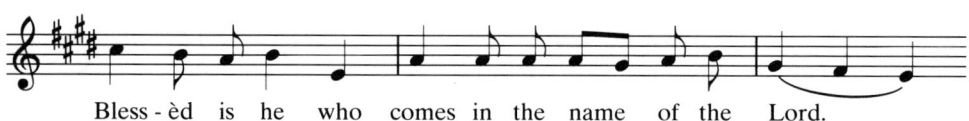

101b Memorial Acclamation

Music: Becket Gerald Senchur, O.S.B. © 1983 St. Vincent Archabbey, Latrobe, PA 15650

Amen 101c

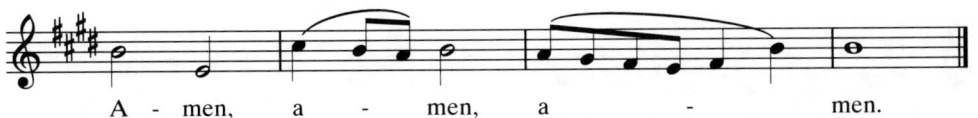

A - men, a - men, a - men.

Lamb of God 101d

Lamb of God, you take a-way the sins of the world: have mer - cy on us.

Lamb of God, you take a-way the sins of the world: grant us peace.

102 EUCHARISTIC ACCLAMATIONS

102a Holy

Ho-ly, ho-ly, ho-ly Lord, God of pow'r and might.

Heav'n and earth are full of your glo-ry. Ho-san-na in the

high-est. Bless-ed is he who comes in the name of the Lord. Ho-

san-na in the high-est. Ho-san-na in the high-est.

102b Memorial Acclamation

Deacon/Celebrant/Cantor
Let us pro-claim the mys-te-ry of faith:

All
Christ has died. Christ is ri-sen. Christ will come a-gain.

102c Amen

A-men, a-men, a-men, a-men.

Music: Isaac Borocz, O.S.B. © 1982 St. Anselm's Abbey, Washington, DC 20017

VERSE 3

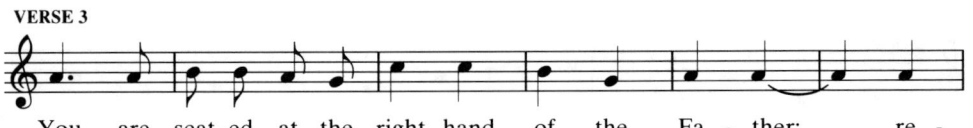

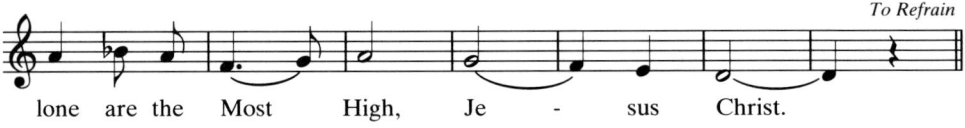

VERSE 4

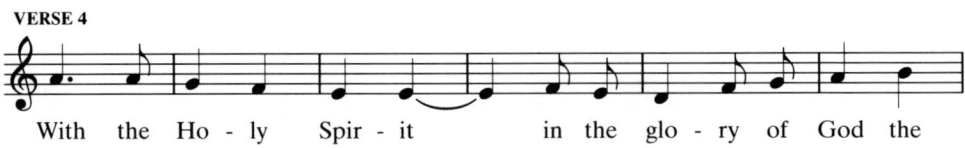

Glory Be to God on High   104

1. Glo - ry be to God on high and peace to all who
2. On - ly Son of God, Lord Je - sus, Lamb of God, A -
3. Je - sus Christ, a - lone Most Ho - ly, One Most High, a -

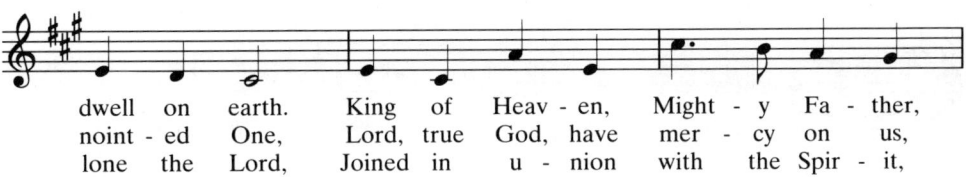

dwell on earth. King of Heav - en, Might - y Fa - ther,
noint - ed One, Lord, true God, have mer - cy on us,
lone the Lord, Joined in u - nion with the Spir - it,

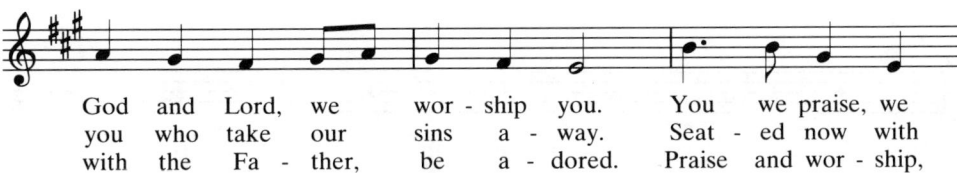

God and Lord, we wor - ship you. You we praise, we
you who take our sins a - way. Seat - ed now with
with the Fa - ther, be a - dored. Praise and wor - ship,

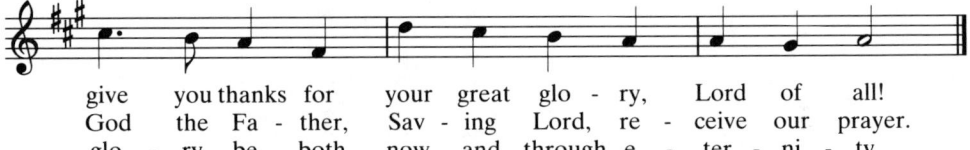

give you thanks for your great glo - ry, Lord of all!
God the Fa - ther, Sav - ing Lord, re - ceive our prayer.
glo - ry be both now and through e - ter - ni - ty.

REGENT SQUARE
87 87 87

Text: Francis R. Muench, O.S.B. © 1985 St. Mary's Abbey, Morristown, NJ 07960

105a Alleluia

105b Alleluia

105c Alleluia

Text: Kilian K. Sullivan, O.S.B. © 1988 Conception Abbey, Conception, MO 64433
Music: Kilian K. Sullivan, O.S.B. © 1988 Conception Abbey, Conception, MO 64433

107 Alleluia. I Call You My Friends
Two-part equal voices

VERSE

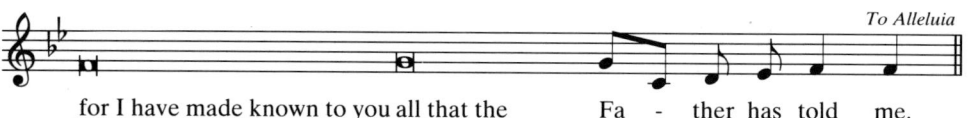

Text: Verse from the LECTIONARY FOR MASS © 1969 ICEL
Music: Jane Klimisch, O.S.B. © 1981 Sacred Heart Convent, Yankton, SD 57578

Alleluia. Your Words, O Lord   108

Text: Verse from the LECTIONARY FOR MASS © 1969 ICEL
Music: Sean Duggan, O.S.B. © 1990 St. Joseph Abbey, St. Benedict, LA 70457

109 Holy (FELICITAS)

Ho - ly, ho - ly, ho - ly Lord,

God of pow - er and of might,

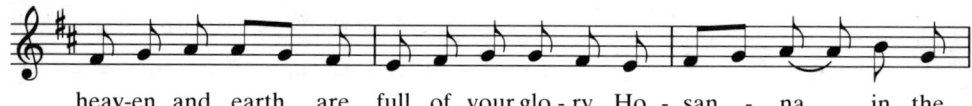
heav-en and earth are full of your glo - ry. Ho - san - na in the

high - est. Bless-ed is he who comes in the name of the

Lord. Ho - san - na in the high - est. Ho -

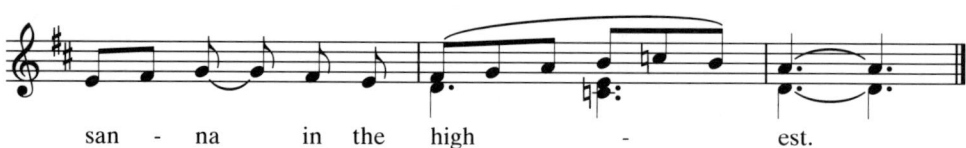
san - na in the high - est.

Music: Becket Gerald Senchur, O.S.B. © 1990 St. Vincent Archabbey, Latrobe, PA 15660

Memorial Acclamation C 110a

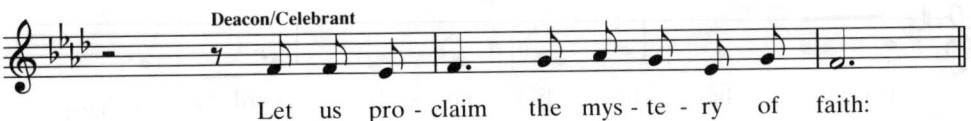
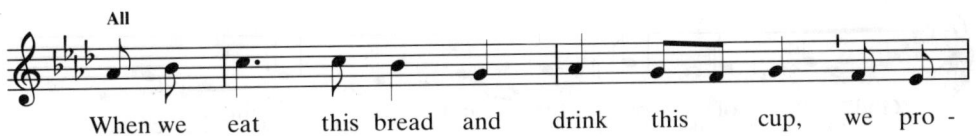

Memorial Acclamation D 110b

Music: Dominic Braud, O.S.B. © 1975 St. Joseph Abbey, St. Benedict, LA 70457; acc. Robert LeBlanc © 1975 St. Joseph Abbey, St. Benedict, LA 70457

111 Lamb of God

Music: Tobias Colgan, O.S.B. © 1985 St. Meinrad Archabbey, St. Meinrad, IN 47577

Lamb of God 112

Music: Becket Gerald Senchur, O.S.B. © 1978 St. Vincent Archabbey, Latrobe, PA 15650

Liturgical Index

CHURCH YEAR

Advent
Come, Let Us to the Lord Our God
Infant Wrapped in God's Own Light
Jesus, Come! For We Invite You
Merciful Redeemer, Come
O Come, Let Us Follow
Oye Nuestra Voz, Oh Cristo
Savior of the Nations, Come
The Word of God
Though the Hills Be Wrapped in Silence
Wait When the Seed Is Planted

Christmas
Christ Is Born to Us This Day
Let Desert Wasteland Now Rejoice
Today Is Born Our Savior
Unto Us a Child Is Given
What Feast of Love

Epiphany
Infant Wrapped in God's Own Light

Lent
Come, Let Us to the Lord Our God
Litany for Lent/Reconciliation
Lord Jesus, As We Turn from Sin
O Father, Lead Us Back to You
Oh Bondadoso Creador, Escucha
Renewed in Your Great Love
We Now Recall the Saving Death
We Stand to Greet the Dawning Day
When Peace Like a River

Passiontide
Out of Everlasting Stillness
There Is No Greater Love
We Now Recall the Saving Death
When Peace Like a River

Holy Thursday
Come, Share This Meal and Eat
In the Breaking of the Bread
  (As We Gather)
Sing of Glory and His Body
Strengthened by the Body and Blood
  of the Lord

Good Friday
We Now Recall the Saving Death

Holy Saturday
I Saw Water Flowing
Now We Gather, Keeping Vigil
Out of Everlasting Stillness

Easter
Alleluia. All Peoples, Clap Your Hands
Hijo del Eterno Padre
I Saw Water Flowing
In the Breaking of the Bread
  (As We Gather)
In the Breaking of the Bread
  (As We Walk)
Into the Silence of Our Hearts
Let Desert Wasteland Now Rejoice
Now We Gather Keeping Vigil
  (verses 3, 4)
Take Courage, Have Faith
This Is the Day the Lord Has Made
Was It Not Needful
When All the Stars of Morning Sang

Pentecost
In the Beginning God Created Heaven
Into the Silence of Our Hearts
Sing, Sing Praise to Creator God
  (verse 3)

Trinity
Day Made Sacred
In the Beginning God Created Heaven
Into the Silence of Our Hearts
O Father, Lead Us Back to You
Out of Everlasting Stillness
Sing, Sing Praise to Creator God

Sacred Heart
Out of Everlasting Stillness

Transfiguration
Lord, It Is Good for Us to Be Here

Church/Dedication
This Is God's Holy Temple

Christ
At This Banquet
Christ Is Born to Us This Day
Hijo del Eterno Padre
I Am the Vine
In the Breaking of the Bread

Infant Wrapped in God's Own Light
Jesus, Come! For We Invite You
Libra Mis Ojos de la Muerte
Lord Jesus Christ, Son of David
Lord Jesus, As We Turn from Sin
Lord, It Is Good for Us to Be Here
Merciful Redeemer, Come
Now We Gather, Keeping Vigil
Oye Nuestra Voz, Oh Cristo
Savior of the Nations, Come
Sing of Glory and His Body
The Lord Said to My Lord
The Word of God
Today Is Born Our Savior
Unto Us a Child Is Given
We Now Recall the Saving Death
You Are the Way
You Are God, We Chant Your Praises

Blessed Virgin Mary
Hail, Mother of Jesus
Hear Our Prayer, O Gentle Mother
I Praise You, O God (Magnificat)
Litany of Mary of Nazareth
Sing We of the Blessed Mother

Saints
Litany of Saints
Lo! What a Cloud of Witnesses
Take Courage, Have Faith
We Praise You, Lord, with Joy This Day
Who Are These, Like Stars Appearing
You Are God, We Chant Your Praises

RITES OF THE CHURCH

Reconciliation
All Who Seek to Know
Come, Let Us to the Lord Our God
I Search and Search to Find My God
Litany for Lent/Reconciliation
Lord Jesus Christ, Son of David
Lord Jesus, As We Turn from Sin
Lord, It Is Good for Us to Be Here
O Come, Let Us Follow
Oh Bondadoso Creador, Escucha
Renewed in Your Great Love
Teach Me the Way of Your Decrees
The Lord Is Kind and Merciful
We Now Recall the Saving Death
When Peace Like a River

Eucharist
   WATER RITE
I Saw Water Flowing
Out of Everlasting Stillness
   GATHERING SONG
Alleluia. All Peoples, Clap Your Hands
Come, Gather at the Table
Day Made Sacred
God of Mercy, God of Grace
God You Call Us to This Place
Great Artist of the Universe
I Rejoiced When I Heard Them Say
Let Us Come Before the Lord
Lord, It Is Good for Us to Be Here
Now We Gather, Keeping Vigil
O Let All That Has Life
Out of Everlasting Stillness
Sing, Sing Praise to Creator God
The Word of God
This Is God's Holy Temple
This Is What the Lord Asks of You
We Come Before You, Lord
You Are the Way
   COMMUNION
At This Banquet
Come, Share This Meal and Eat
I Am the Vine
In the Breaking of the Bread
Jesus, Come! For We Invite You
Let the Hungry Come to Me
Lord, You Are a Banquet
Merciful Redeemer, Come
Sing of Glory and His Body
Strengthened by the Body and Blood
  of the Lord
The Cup of Salvation
To the Wedding Feast God Calls Us
What Feast of Love
   RECESSIONAL
Not in the Wind
Now Go, the Mass Is Ended
O Let All That Has Life
On Our Journey to the Kingdom
Sing, Sing Praise to Creator God
This Is the Day the Lord Has Made
We Thank You Father, Lord of All
You Are the Way

Wake/Funeral
All Who Seek to Know
Good and Faithful Servant
I Rejoiced When I Head Them Say

If a Grain of Wheat Falls
Libra Mis Ojos de la Muerte
Litany for Lent/Reconciliation
Lo! What a Cloud of Witnesses
Lord, You Are a Banquet
The Lord Is Kind and Merciful
We Offer Prayer in Sorrow, Lord
We Praise You, Lord, with Joy This Day
We Thank You, Father, Lord of All
When from Bondage We Are Summoned

Litany
Litany for Lent/Reconciliation
Litany of Mary of Nazareth
Litany of Saints

LITURGY OF THE HOURS

Morning Prayer
Alabemos a Dios
Come, Let Us to the Lord Our God
Cuándo, Señor, Te Llevarás Cautiva
Day Made Sacred
En la Noche las Sombras Oscuras
God of Mercy, God of Grace
In the Beginning God Created Heaven
Lord, It Is Good for Us to Be Here
Though the Hills Be Wrapped in Silence
We Praise You, Lord, with Joy This Day
We Stand to Greet the Dawning Day
We Thank You, Father, Lord of All
When All the Stars of Morning Sang

Evening Prayer
As Evening Falls
Day Made Sacred
I Praise You, O God (Magnificat)

I Search and Search to Find My God
Libra Mis Ojos de la Muerte
Lord Jesus, As We Turn from Sin
Lord, It Is Good for Us to Be Here
Not in the Wind
O Come, Bless the Lord
The Blazing Sun Has Run Its Course
Wait When the Seed Is Planted
When Evening Falls and Labors Cease

Psalms
9	There Is No Greater Love
24 (25)	Let Everything Within You
30	Take Courage, Have Faith
33	Was It Not Needful
46 (47)	Alleluia. All Peoples, Clap Your Hands
63	I Search and Search To Find My God
62 (63)	Lord, You Are a Banquet
67	God of Mercy
84	Good and Faithful Servant
96	Today Is Born Our Savior
100 (101)	This Is What the Lord Asks of You
102 (103)	The Lord Is Kind and Merciful
110	The Lord Said to My Lord
115 (116)	The Cup of Salvation
118	Let Us Come Before the Lord
119	Teach Me the Way of Your Decrees
121 (122)	I Rejoiced When I Heard Them Say
134	O Come, Bless the Lord
138	If a Grain of Wheat Falls

Topical Index

Beatitudes
We Come Before You, Lord

Commissioning
Not in the Wind
On Our Journey to the Kingdom
This Is What the Lord Asks of You

Commitment
We Stand to Greet the Dawning Day

Conversion
Alabemos a Dios
Almighty God, Your Word Is Cast
Cuándo, Señor, Te Llevarás Cautiva
Lord Jesus, As We Turn from Sin
Lord, It Is Good for Us to Be Here
O Come, Let Us Follow
O Father, Lead Us Back to You
Teach Me the Way of Your Decrees
The Lord Is Kind and Merciful

Creation
Great Artist of the Universe
In the Beginning God Created Heaven
Jesus, Come! For We Invite You
Not in the Wind
O Let All That Has Life
Sing, Sing Praise to Creator God
Though the Hills Be Wrapped in Silence
Wait When the Seed Is Planted
We Thank You, Father, Lord of All
When All the Stars of Morning Sang
You Are God, We Chant Your Praises

Cross
Sing of Glory and His Body
We Now Recall the Saving Death
When Peace Like a River

Faith
I Search and Search to Find My God
Libra Mis Ojos de la Muerte
Lord, It Is Good for Us to Be Here
Not in the Wind
Take Courage, Have Faith
This Is God's Holy Temple
Wait When the Seed Is Planted
You Are the Way

Healing
Cuando, Señor, Te Llevarás Cautiva
Libra Mis Ojos de la Muerte

Lord Jesus, As We Turn from Sin
The Word of God

Hope
All Who Seek to Know
Come, Let Us to the Lord Our God
Jesus, Come! For We Invite You
Let Desert Wasteland Now Rejoice
Not in the Wind
O Father, Lead Us Back to You
Savior of the Nations, Come
Though the Hills Be Wrapped in Silence
Today Is Born Our Savior
Unto Us a Child Is Given
Wait When the Seed Is Planted

Journey
In the Breaking of the Bread
 (As We Walk)
O Come, Let Us Follow
On Our Journey to the Kingdom
When from Bondage We Are Summoned

Joy
Alleluia. All Peoples, Clap Your Hands
Let Desert Wasteland Now Rejoice
O Let All That Has Life

Jubilee
The Cup of Salvation

Justice
Cuándo, Señor, Te Llevarás Cautiva
I Praise You, O God (Magnificat)
Let the Hungry Come to Me
Litany of Mary of Nazareth
This Is What the Lord Asks of You
We Come Before You, Lord
When Peace Like a River

Light
In the Beginning God Created Heaven
Infant Wrapped in God's Own Light
Savior of the Nations, Come
Though the Hills Be Wrapped in Silence

Love
Lord, It Is Good for Us to Be Here
Sing, Sing Praise to Creator God
Strengthened by the Body and Blood
 of the Lord
We Now Recall the Saving Death

Mercy
All Who Seek to Know
God of Mercy, God of Grace
Lord Jesus Christ, Son of David
The Lord Is Kind and Merciful
This Is What the Lord Asks of You

Ministry
Not in the Wind
This Is What the Lord Asks of You

Peace—see Justice

People of God
Alabemos a Dios
God, You Call Us to This Place
I Am the Vine
This Is God's Holy Temple

Perseverance
Good and Faithful Servant
Libra Mis Ojos de la Muerte

Petition
Cuándo, Señor, Te Llevarás Cautiva
Jesus, Come! For We Invite You
Teach Me the Way of Your Decrees

Pilgrimage
O Come, Let Us Follow
On Our Journey to the Kingdom
When from Bondage We Are Summoned

Praise
Alabemos a Dios
God of Mercy, God of Grace
Great Artist of the Universe
I Praise You, O God (Magnificat)
Let Us Come Before the Lord
Lord, You Are a Banquet
O Let All That Has Life
Sing, Sing Praise to Creator God
Take Courage, Have Faith
There Is No Greater Love
You Are God, We Chant Your Praises

Presence of God
Infant Wrapped in God's Own Light
Strengthened by the Body and Blood
 of the Lord
We Come Before You, Lord

Profession of Vows
If a Grain of Wheat Falls
The Cup of Salvation
This Is What the Lord Asks of You

Redemption—see Salvation

Renewal
When All the Stars of Morning Sang

Responsibility
Almighty God, Your Word Is Cast
This Is What the Lord Asks of You

Retreat
Not in the Wind

Salvation
Christ Is Born to Us This Day
Merciful Redeemer, Come
Sing of Glory and His Body
We Now Recall the Saving Death
We Thank You, Father, Lord of All
When Peace Like a River

Service
Almighty God, Your Word Is Cast
Good and Faithful Servant
Teach Me the Way of Your Decrees
There Is No Greater Love

Social Concerns
I Praise You, O God
Let the Hungry Come to Me
Libra Mis Ojos de la Muerte
Litany of Mary of Nazareth
We Come Before You, Lord

Thanksgiving
God of Mercy, God of Grace
Great Artist of the Universe
If a Grain of Wheat Falls
Let Us Come Before the Lord
The Lord Is Kind and Merciful
We Thank You, Father, Lord of All
You Are God, We Chant Your Praises

Trust
Jesus, Come! For We Invite You
O Come, Let Us Follow
Wait When the Seed Is Planted
You Are the Way

Unity
God, You Call Us to This Place
Strengthened by the Body and Blood
 of the Lord

Word of God
Alabemos a Dios
Almighty God, Your Word Is Cast
God, You Call Us to This Place
Lord, It Is Good for Us to Be Here
Teach Me the Way of Your Decrees
The Word of God